MARY RD

The boy, the bike and the fish truck

© Day One 2023
First printed 2023

ISBN 978-1-84625-748-3

British Library Cataloguing in Publication Data available

All opinions and endorsements expressed in this book regarding running aids are solely the author's and do not necessarily reflect the views of Day One Publications.

Published by Day One Publications
Ryelands Road, Leominster, HR6 8NZ
email—sales@dayone.co.uk
web site—www.dayone.co.uk

Cover illustration by Kathryn Chedgzoy
Printed by 4edge

Dedication

For Kabanda, Florence and family.

Thank you for your friendship and love.

May you always be surrounded by God's love and peace.

Kabanda in 2007

Contents

1 Kabanda

It was evening, and the tropical sun had set, spreading its brilliance across the sky. I could hear the frogs croaking, sounding like an army of old men snoring. I should have left the balcony and retreated into the living room before the mosquitoes made a meal of me, but I wanted a few more minutes alone with this remarkable young man.

'These are my results so far, Aunt,' he respectfully told me. 'I still have one more result to come, but I felt that that exam went well, so I do not worry.'

I looked at Kabanda Nelson and said quietly, 'I am so proud of you!'

'So am I,' echoed a deep voice behind me, and I looked round to see Hugh Henderson, Kabanda's adoptive father, standing behind us. We looked at each other and smiled. We knew what a great achievement this was; indeed, it was a miracle that his boy had gained a BA.

On that evening, in August 2005, we were together in Kigali, Rwanda. Kabanda is a Ugandan young man and had travelled by bus from Uganda to be with us and join our mission team. Hugh was at that time the mission director for a small Christian charity with whom I was also working as a volunteer. It was through Hugh that I had first met Kabanda in 2002, when we were on a trip together and he had invited his adoptive son to join us.

From our first meeting, I was impressed by this young man, and when I heard his story, I was so moved by it and was sure that it needed sharing with the wider world. It was a Good Samaritan story for this generation, for this century.

Kabanda was born into a strongly Muslim family on 4 September 1981. The family lived in a village in the Mukono district of Uganda, where 98% of the population were followers of the Islamic religion and traditions. It was a large family, Kabanda being one of thirteen children born to his father and the seventh son born into the family. His birth was the only one of the family's that had occurred during the holy month of Ramadan, so there was great celebration and joy that he should be such an honoured child.

There was also great disappointment, for his father had been longing for a daughter to be born. Kabanda's mother was his third wife; the previous two wives had been divorced because they had failed to produce the much longed-for daughter. Kabanda's mother, although a Muslim, also held very strongly to the traditional belief in ancestral spirits. Through many years of misfortunes, her sacrificing to and consulting with these spirits did not appear to help her in any way, but she continued to hold to these beliefs.

As a new bride, once she realised that she was pregnant, she knew that it was important to produce a female child in order to preserve her marriage. Cultural belief taught that it was the mother who determined the sex of the unborn child, so knowing she had conceived, she immediately went to consult the traditional doctors. The correct sacrifices were made to the ancestral spirits and considerable payment given to the witch doctor, so she returned satisfied and assured by the 'doctor' that she was pregnant with the greatly longed-for daughter. She convinced Kabanda's father that she was carrying a baby girl, and he treated her with special favours throughout the pregnancy. Together they waited for the birth of this special daughter.

When the time for delivery drew near, Kabanda's father even stopped working so that he could be near and would be the first to see the longed-for baby girl. This was a difficult thing for a man to do when he earned so little and had a big family to feed, but it was so important to him to have a daughter. All the clothes, and even some toys that had been prepared for the baby, were for a girl.

The time for the delivery came, and the disappointment of the birth of yet another son was very great, yet the fact that he was born in the holy month could not be ignored. Kabanda's mother, in order to defend herself, explained the situation by saying that she had indeed been pregnant with a baby girl, but for some reason the ancestors were displeased with the family, so in the delivery a boy appeared. She viewed her little son as some sort of terrible birth accident and was never able to give to him the maternal love that all children need.

She did conceive again, and her secondborn was a girl, so Kabanda eventually had a sister. However, even when her daughter had been born, Kabanda's mother could not find it in her heart to forgive him for being a boy and could not bring herself to love him.

There was one person, however, who was very thrilled when Kabanda was born, and that was his paternal grandmother. She was a very staunch Muslim who could always be found praying on Fridays and even as a very old woman still kept the fast of Ramadan. She felt that this special child born within the holy month must be nurtured in the Islamic faith and did all she could to encourage this. She sensed he had a special destiny since he had been favoured in this way, so from time to time as Kabanda grew up, she would give him gifts of

Islamic clothing. She praised him above all his brothers and later, sisters, born into her son's family. He was her 'Joseph' in this large family. Her attention made up a little for the lack of a mother's love.

Kabanda remembers fondly how very much she loved him. She was always introducing him to very faithful Muslim friends to encourage him in the faith.

The family were extremely poor. As practising Muslims, they had been taught that it was their duty to produce as many children as possible, even though they did not have the capacity to feed, clothe or educate them all. As more and more children were born into the home, it became increasingly difficult to feed them. They all knew what it felt like to go to bed hungry, but that was the experience of most people who lived around them, and they accepted it all as the will of Allah.

The family owned a shamba, or plantation, but it was a poor piece of land, even though quite large. It was dry and arid, and the parents worked hard to try and grow crops on it for the family. Season by season, they would plough and till the ground, hoping to cultivate more crops. Every year they hoped and prayed it would become more fertile. Through their ignorance of agriculture and the infertility of the ground, they were not able to increase the yield of crops, and they therefore assumed that in some way they must have displeased the ancestral spirits.

To try to help the situation at the beginning of each season, the parents would sacrifice a chicken as a way of praying to the spirits for a good harvest. The loss of livestock in this way impoverished the family even further. Poverty became a way of life and hunger a constant companion. Rather than accepting it was futile to consult the spirits, Kabanda's mother lived in fear and bondage to them.

The family's circumstances grew worse each year.

2 Consulting the witch doctor

One incident made a deep impression on Kabanda as he grew up. The family situation was going from bad to worse financially, so Kabanda's father decided to consult the spirits himself to find out why they were not favouring his family. His occupation was tailoring. He was too poor to rent his own premises in which to run his business, but a friend allowed him to use the large veranda outside of his shop to set up and use his sewing machine there. He gave this friend a gift each month from his wages, and the small income he made supplemented the shamba in feeding the family.

The veranda was large, and eventually another tailor also began working there. The competition soon caused problems. The new tailor was able to sew more fashionable clothes and began to acquire many customers, including those who had previously patronised Kabanda's father. This reduced the family income yet further, causing increased poverty and famine to the family. Something had to be done! Why were the spirits so displeased?

There was only one way to find out. The family had to consult a powerful witch doctor. There was one who came from Tanzania who had a great reputation particularly for solving work problems. His name was Dr Maji Moto (Dr Water of Fire), and he still operates in the area.

Kabanda's father took three cocks, some eggs and a sum of money and went to the shrine to consult this witch doctor. He explained the situation of the new tailor coming to work on the veranda and how he was losing even the little business he had.

'Don't worry, my son,' was the reassuring reply from Dr Maji Moto. 'You have come to the right place. Your troubles are over.'

Kabanda's father was invited to enter the shrine so that rituals could be performed over him. Two of the cocks were slaughtered over his head in order that the blood could run down him and wash away his misfortunes. He was then forbidden to wash for the next three days so that the blood stains would remain powerfully on his body. He was told to return home and not to return to work for a further nine days.

Kabanda remembers his father returning home, stinking with the smell of stale chicken blood and looking very miserable and distressed. Although he still felt very worried about the family situation and had no real hope inside himself that it would improve, he continued to obey Dr Maji Moto's instruction and kept away from work for a further nine days. When he did return to town, it was to discover that he had now lost his few remaining customers, since they thought he had quit his job. They had defected to the new tailor!

This became a turning point in the life of Kabanda's father, for he vowed never again to consult a witch doctor. He declared he would call on God to help him from then on, although he did not confess the way to God through the cross of Christ or practise any Christian faith. Looking back, Kabanda thanks God for this incident, which released his father from believing in the witch doctor, even though his mother continued to do so.

Although Kabanda never enjoyed the love and nurture from his mother that is every child's birthright, he knew that his father loved him. This comforted and sustained him through some of the hard times. There was always, of course, a deep longing that perhaps, one day, his mother would have a change of heart towards him.

Things were far from easy for Kabanda growing up in the family. One day, when he was only six years old, his mother sent him on an errand to the pharmacy. It was quite a long way for a little boy to walk. He was to buy some Maxadol. In order to remember what he was to buy, he began to sing the word, chanting it in a song—'Maxadol, Maxadol, Maxadol!'—as he walked along the dusty path. However, on the way a neighbour stopped him, and they exchanged greetings. It is the custom to stop and greet everyone you know when you are walking along the road, so Kabanda was not being naughty when he did this. He would have been very rude if he had not stopped.

However, when he started his journey again, he found it hard to remember the song that he had made up in order to get the correct medicine for his mother. The only word he could remember was of another drug used at times in the home, so he began singing, 'Panadol, Panadol, Panadol!'

The errand completed, Kabanda ran home. His mother was extremely angry with him because he had brought home the wrong drug. Although he was only a little boy of six, she punished him by locking him in the small room where the chickens were housed. It had no ventilation and was very dark.

'You are as stupid as the chickens who laid their eggs in the neighbour's place,' she shouted as she locked him in, leaving him there without food or water. Kabanda stayed, crouched in fear, stuck in that unpleasant place all day. It was both very dark and hot, and he was terrified. When his father came home from work in the evening and found he was there, he quickly let him out. This punishment was typical of his mother's attitude towards him. It seemed she could not find love and compassion for him.

There was one day when she was pleased with Kabanda and proud of him! It happened when he was attending primary school. Kabanda loved school and studied well. He pleased his teachers because he was well behaved and hardworking.

One year he demonstrated such good behaviour and his results were so brilliant that on Parents' Day his mother was called out in front of everybody because Kabanda had been honoured. He had won a prize, which was that the school promised to pay his school fees for the next term, and on top of that, his class teacher had given him a new school uniform.

That day Kabanda's mother was very happy with her son and promised to buy him a pencil sharpener for the new term. Kabanda was delighted and felt he was loved, so he determined to work even harder. Indeed, he made a promise to himself that he would always be the best pupil in the class. He probably would have achieved this aim had he not often through the years been sent home from school because the fees had not been paid.

He never did get the pencil sharpener his mother had promised to buy for him. From time to time, he would remind his mother, but she replied, 'You'll have to wait until I go to the city.' Whether she really intended to buy it for him, we shall never know, but it was a great disappointment to Kabanda. A pencil sharpener would have been a prized possession to a little child who lived in such a poor family.

3 Family matters

Kabanda had six older brothers. As a small child, he longed for their attention and friendship and to play with them. Sadly, they had no feelings of affection for him. From their point of view, they felt that his mother had been the reason why their father had divorced their mothers. Indeed, apart from the brother who was closest to him in age, they held animosity towards him, and he felt very isolated.

In African culture, family members are seen as belonging together and continue to live in close proximity even though there has been divorce and remarriage. It would have been normal for children with different mothers to have been brought up as brothers, playing and living together. Kabanda was able to play sometimes with the youngest of the six, but even he was not kind and loving towards Kabanda. This really made him sad, especially as his mother had so little time for him.

The village in which they lived was a collection of small mud houses, and everyone was very poor. The school in the village had low standards, and the teaching was very rudimentary. There was no help for any child to reach his potential. At the completion of primary seven, it was expected that a child would be able to sign his own name and reply in English, 'I'm fine!' when greeted. Those two things were supposed to equip him for adult life!

It could also take many years to complete primary seven, as at the end of each year children were required to sit and pass a national examination before progressing to the next class. Because so many children only went to school when there was enough money to pay even the small amount needed for the fees, they struggled to learn enough to pass the required exams and progress to the next class.

Kabanda's father made the situation very clear to all his sons. They had to attend primary school, because that was legally required by the government, but once having completed primary seven, there certainly would be no money for secondary education.

This is what happened to Kabanda's six older brothers. As soon as they finished primary school, they left school and were expected to work on the family shamba through the three months' holiday in order to repay the family for the sacrifice in sending them to school, and then they had to look for a place to live away from the family home. Most of them went to the nearest town to start an independent life.

It was not easy for these boys to get any form of employment, and certainly they had no prospects of a career. Little more than children, they had to compete for jobs in an adult world and somehow get enough money to buy food and shelter. Life is so hard for the children brought up in poverty, and they have very little hope that their lives could ever change for the better.

Within Kabanda was always a longing to study. He had a great desire to go to secondary school. As he grew up, it seemed as if circumstances were going to make this possible.

Kabanda's parents had adopted James as an eight-year-old orphan, into their family. James himself never had the opportunity to go to school but lived with the family until he was fifteen. After leaving the family home, James began employment in the forest as a timber worker. He felt that by caring for the younger Kabanda, sixteen years his junior, he could repay the debt he owed to the family who had taken him in. His work took him away for three months at a time, and each time he returned he brought Kabanda gifts like shoes, T-shirts, pens, notebooks and even the longed-for pencil sharpener! He acted like a parent to Kabanda and always loved and cared for him. When James was twenty, he married. Sadly, his wife had already been infected with HIV. After a short while, she became pregnant and gave birth to a baby daughter.

Two weeks after the birth of this little girl, the mother died. Kabanda went to live with James and took care of the baby while James was at work, but very sadly she too died after six months. Kabanda felt the loss of James's wife and daughter deeply as well as feeling sorrowful for James.

James had always promised that he would pay secondary school fees for Kabanda, but by now James was infected with the same terrible virus and went into decline after the tragic death of his wife and child. He even refused the drugs which might have prolonged his life. So Kabanda suffered the loss of the family whom he cared about and the home where he had felt loved and secure. With James's death, he also lost hope of continuing at school.

However, after James's death, Kabanda still had a great longing to continue his education and felt he wanted to honour his friend by somehow attending at least the first year of secondary school. He talked to his father about his feelings and managed to persuade him to allow Kabanda to use a corner of their land to make bricks from the fine red clay. His father's reply was unexpectedly encouraging: 'Son, yes, you may use the ground to make bricks, and I will also lend you my mould to make them.'

The wooden mould to shape the bricks would make a huge difference, and Kabanda spent his entire three months' holiday, day after day, in the repetitive task of making one brick after the other. He made mud from the clay by digging a hole and mixing the earth with water, then putting it into a mould and allowing each brick to set. The brick was then turned out and allowed to dry in the sunshine. It was a slow, laborious task, working outside all day in the heat of the sun. All the while, he had to bear the scorn and ridicule of his older brothers and school friends, who thought he was crazy to work in this way.

'Forget it!' they jeered at him day after day. 'You'll never make enough bricks to get school fees! Forget school—come and play football, you stupid idiot!'

However, his persistent labour paid off. At the end of the holiday, Kabanda sold his sun-dried bricks and raised 60,000 Ugandan shillings (£20). This enabled him to register at secondary school and pay for the first two terms!

After Kabanda managed to accomplish this, it brought further bitter jealousy, anger and hatred from his brothers so that his life became more difficult than ever. He had so little encouragement from his family. No one seemed to appreciate his determination and hard work or his ambition to learn.

Partly because of the worsening situation in the family, Kabanda asked his maternal aunt if he could stay at her home and attend secondary school from there. She lived in another town some distance from the family home, and she had taken some interest in the lad from time to time, recognising that her sister had rejected him.

Kabanda's father gave him an old bicycle as his contribution towards his son's future. Although he had never ridden a bike before, Kabanda bravely pedalled the 45 km to the town where his aunt lived, carrying his few belongings in a polythene bag.

He was only fourteen years old. There was no loving send-off from the family, no best wishes for his future or pride in this son who was determined to make something of his life!

It was a traumatic journey for him, for he didn't know the way and had to keep stopping and asking people the route. Indeed, the trip took him the whole day, and an exhausted youth finally arrived at his aunt's home. He arrived hot, dusty and just a bit nervous of what might lie ahead.

Everything was different, and very strange. Life was still hard, although no worse than in his own home. Kabanda knew that his aunt cared for him, for in the past she had tried to compensate a little for the lack of love he had received from his mother. She had always joked with her sister that she was a better parent because Kabanda loved her the most!

Her husband had not wanted Kabanda to come and stay with them, but she had convinced him that the lad would not eat too much, so in the end he agreed.

The boy, the bike and the fish truck

4 Secondary school

The following week, Kabanda went to the secondary school to register himself as a pupil. This was in itself quite a big step for the boy to take alone. He had his hard-earned cash in his pocket to pay for his first two terms. He of course needed writing materials and a uniform, all of which he was required to provide for himself, but he had his bicycle that his father had given him, and that was his proud possession as it was his best means of earning the extra money so that he could keep himself.

Only the English language was permitted to be spoken in the school, and Kabanda did not know any English, having spent his years at such a poor primary school where only a very few words had been taught. This made life difficult and especially hard for Kabanda to make friends and settle down. To be suddenly not allowed to speak in your own mother tongue and to be almost unable to understand anything which the teachers or pupils were saying put Kabanda at a real place of disadvantage. He was determined that having got this far, he was not going to be defeated, so he tried very hard to cope.

Eventually he made a friend called Frank. Although Frank had attended a good primary school, he struggled to learn English, so they spoke together in the mother tongue of Luganda. This helped the friendship to flourish.

'I don't have words to describe how I felt on my first day at the school,' Kabanda told me when he was relating his story. 'I was so happy, and it felt really great to be in a secondary school.'

Chapter 4

The first task was to read the school rules and regulations and to sign that you would abide by them. Kabanda was willing to do that, even though one of the rules said that only English must be spoken all day in and around the school compound.

Another rule said that there was to be no leaving school until it closed, which happened quite late in the evening. This was a problem as it conflicted with his aunt's plans to make him work to repay her hospitality. She meant for him to fetch water, do the housework and do the shopping in the market using his bike! She didn't expect to put a roof over the head of her nephew for nothing; indeed, she saw a great opportunity for some unpaid help!

Somehow Kabanda managed to fit these tasks around his school day and use his bicycle to earn a little money for himself as well. He would be up at daybreak around 6:00 a.m. and do the chores for his aunt, like fetching water. He would then go to the market and offer to transport other people's shopping, carrying it to their homes on his bike. The small amount of money he earned enabled him to buy the necessities for school and help with food. It was hard work, but he persevered.

Sometimes people would take advantage of him. One day a very large man asked him to transport him, using the bicycle as a taxi. Kabanda was not sure where the place was that the man wanted to visit but agreed to do it. The man paid a small amount for the fare, and they began the journey.

It was much, much further than either the man had indicated or Kabanda had anticipated, and the man sitting on the back of the bike became heavier and heavier, so that in the end, it was impossible for Kabanda to pedal any more. He kept going for as long as he could, and then darkness fell, and an exhausted young Kabanda had to stop. He told the man he could go no further. The man then demanded all the fare be returned to him as Kabanda had not taken him all the way! When Kabanda argued with him about this, the man insisted that he pedal the bike, and they continued the journey this way.

They rode deep into the forest, then the man slapped Kabanda over the head, stole the bicycle and rode away. Kabanda started to shout and call for help, but there was no one around to hear him. It was pitch dark in the forest, with only the noise of insects and small creatures echoing around him. He was frightened and distressed as he started the long, long walk back home, crying all the way. It was a terrible experience for such a young boy, and it was very late at night when he finally arrived at his aunt's home.

When Kabanda finally lay on his bed, he was unable to sleep because he couldn't stop thinking about the huge loss of his bicycle. It was his treasured possession, his only means of transport and income. Now his problems had doubled overnight. How could he earn money for food and school requirements, let alone save for further school fees? Up until that time, he had not managed to save anything because people had only paid him a pittance for his work as they perceived he was just a boy. It was a devastating thing to have happened to him.

However, life had to go on, and the next morning Kabanda had to get up and do his chores and then walk to school. He felt very dispirited. At school he confided to his friend Frank about what had happened to him. It was a loss for Frank too, for although his father used to drive him to school each morning, Kabanda would take him home at the end of the day on the back of his bike.

Walking to school and back presented no real problem, as children in Uganda are used to walking long distances, but having no means to earn money for food was a major obstacle for Kabanda. Since the customers at the market were still looking for him, a solution presented itself to this resourceful young boy. He would walk with the packages on his head! It was not easy with a small head and small legs, but he still persevered.

Frank was really touched when he saw what Kabanda was doing. He decided to talk to his father about it.

'Well, son, we'll see what we can do,' was the response from a compassionate heart. Frank's father must have truly been a remarkable man, because he cared so much that he bought Kabanda a brand-new bicycle! Kabanda was overwhelmed with joy! To have a new bicycle, one that was not forever breaking down because it was on its last wheels!

Kabanda was only fourteen years old and working far harder than any young child should. Many people who had got to know him respected and sympathised with him and wanted to help by offering him full-time employment if he wanted to give up studying. They saw a young person who was both determined to succeed and not afraid of hard work. One job he was offered was to be a taxi conductor, and although this was an attractive proposition, Kabanda was determined to finish at least one year of secondary school, so he declined.

All these months he stayed at his aunt's house, but life there was not easy either. Kabanda no longer bothered to attend the mosque because he was realising that this God he had been brought up to worship was not a kind God. Even though he felt that Islam was an empty religion, he had no desire to listen to Christian teaching or seek God in any other way. He just felt it was all a waste of time and had no real meaning.

Within the first few months of Kabanda living in his aunt's home, her husband became very sick and died from AIDS, leaving the responsibility of care for many children to his wife. Kabanda's aunt worked in the market, where she was very poorly paid, and she was left quite unable to care for all the household. After her husband's funeral, she could not work for a whole month as she was grieving deeply, and this left Kabanda with the responsibility of providing food for all the family, using his new bicycle to earn money.

It was a terrible time, and in the end Kabanda felt he had no option but to leave school and find full-time work. It was just before the examinations at the end of the second term. Having agonised over the problems and come to this decision, he shared it with his friend, Frank. He would do the exams, but then leave. That way, at least he would have something to show for the effort and work of the past few months. He had done his best; he had tried.

The remaining problem was how to raise the money to pay the exam fees. It was then that Kabanda decided to return to his home village and ask his natural parents for the money. There was a slim chance that they would be able to help him this one last time. He would ride all the way to Mukono and ask his father for the fees.

5 The first accident

I t was 20 August 1996. The morning was cool and pleasant, and Kabanda was glad for this as he began the long bicycle ride back to his family home in Mukono. It made the journey so much easier, and he could pedal more quickly. He had to negotiate a lot of traffic on the main road, but at least the surface was tarmac. As he travelled, he turned over in his mind how he should ask his father for the money.

When his father saw Kabanda, he was covered with embarrassment.

'My son,' he said, 'I am so sorry that I have neglected you for so long!' He welcomed his son with enthusiasm and invited him in. That warmed Kabanda's heart and encouraged him to make his request. Somehow it was such a relief to open his heart and relate to his father all that had happened through the past months since he had left home.

Kabanda began to tell him the story of his time at school. So much had happened in just a few months. The young boy who had cycled so timidly to start secondary school had begun to be confident and mature. He was becoming a man.

His father agreed with the idea that once he had sat the exams it would be good to pack his bags and go to the capital city, Kampala, and find work. Now that he could speak a little English and knew a little more of the world, he surely would be able to get a job.

'Perhaps the taxi driver still needs a conductor!' Kabanda's father encouraged him.

His father was able to give him the money he needed to pay for the examination.

Kabanda had really enjoyed the day with his father, but since he had his exams the following morning, he said goodbye and began the journey back to his aunt's home. It was a long way to ride, and he didn't want to be too late getting there.

He had only been cycling for about a kilometre when it began to rain. It was not just a drizzle but the sort of rain that drenches a person instantly, as only tropical rain can do! In Uganda the paths become a red, muddy slide within minutes, and even the paved roads have water rushing down the gullies on both sides of them. All driving and cycling soon becomes very difficult. Kabanda was soaking wet, but he had to continue the journey because he could not miss his exams the next day, so he struggled on through the driving rain and poor visibility.

Conditions deteriorated more and more as he pedalled, and then suddenly he was hit by a vehicle travelling behind him. It was a fish lorry, and so great was the impact that the truck overturned. The driver scrambled out of his cab and went over to look at the person he had hit. He saw an unconscious little heap of humanity, and he felt sure that the person was already dead, so he left him where he was and went at once to the nearest police post to report the accident and ask them to remove the body. This was the story he told the police when he reported the accident. No other witnesses ever came forward, and Kabanda was unconscious, so perhaps the whole truth will never be known.

Kabanda had been thrown into the culvert that was full of water. He was unconscious and dying, with no one around to help. There were people only too willing to gain from the accident, stealing Kabanda's clothes and leaving him only in his underpants, and of course they took the money his father had given him. As they stripped him, they must have realised that he was still breathing, though badly injured, but they just left him there to die. The cold water in the culvert where he had been propelled was swirling around him and almost drowning him. The dark red muddy water was now bloodstained.

There were also other people who were taking advantage of the overturned fish truck and helping themselves to free dinners! It seemed to them more important to steal a fish or two for supper than to help this severely wounded young person.

'God's ways are beyond understanding, and He looks out for the most crucial moments to show His love,' said Kabanda as he related his story.

Driving along the road that night were two Scotsmen who were in Uganda for a short-term preaching mission. They were returning after a frustrating evening. Having arrived at a village where they were supposed to preach that evening, they had found the church closed and so there was no congregation. They later found the pastor at his home. He was sick with a bout of malaria. It had seemed like a wasted day, and then, as they were returning to their base, it began to rain.

The rain was so heavy that it was almost impossible to see the road ahead, but suddenly they came upon a lorry that had turned onto its side, and many people were crowded around it. Then the headlights picked up a tangled mass of metal, and Hugh Henderson, who was driving, realised that it was the remains of a bicycle.

They stopped the car and looked to see if they could help. It was then that Hugh spotted the body in the culvert. He too thought it was a corpse, but when he went closer to look, he realised the boy was still, if only just, alive.

Gently, the two men wrapped the dying boy in a coat and carried him into the back of the car. From his case, Hugh extracted a towel and wrapped it around the mangled, fractured leg. They doubted that he would make it in time but drove as quickly as they were able in the wet conditions back to Kampala and to Mulago Hospital.

Kabanda has no recollection of what happened next. He only remembers gaining consciousness at some point and seeing his bed surrounded with doctors in white coats and an enormous 'mzungu' (white person) who looked so happy when he opened his eyes. Kabanda thought he must have woken up in heaven and that perhaps this man was God!

All Kabanda was able to remember was that he had left home to cycle back to school. At least he had some memory, which encouraged the doctors in thinking that his brain was not badly damaged.

'What has happened to me? Why am I here?' he asked.

'You have been in a traffic accident, and now you are in Mulago Hospital,' was the reply Hugh gave him.

Kabanda thought that the mzungu was lying to him, because he felt no pain. He decided to sit up on the bed, but when he tried, he realised his arm would not move. He tried again and then saw his leg with the blood-soaked towel around it and the bone sticking out!

The arm was also badly fractured at the shoulder, and there were several cuts and contusions to the head and body. He also realised he was naked, and so his clothes and presumably all his money had been stolen. As he lay there, his condition began to sink in. Things were bad!

Lying in the hospital, Kabanda was given good attention because he had been brought there by a white person, and this man had stayed to see he was treated properly. Hugh's continued concern saved this young boy's life, for without money he would not have been treated. Government hospitals in Uganda give only very basic care to patients who have no money or are not under some kind of healthcare scheme. Poor people such as Kabanda's family had nothing, so without Hugh's help, Kabanda would not have received proper care.

Kabanda drifted in and out of consciousness, feeling, as he described himself, 'like someone who has journeyed 1,000 miles on foot.' When he was more fully awake, Hugh asked him his name.

'Ramathan,' Kabanda answered, and promptly fell asleep again. Ramathan was his Muslim forename.

The next recollection Kabanda has of that time is that Hugh gently stretched his hand over his head and started praying for him. Kabanda remembers being moved by the words and feeling peace come over him. Hugh spoke as if there was a dear friend next to him, and Kabanda heard words that sounded like 'my Lord Jesus,' and he realised that Hugh must be a Christian because Christians worshipped Jesus.

Until that time, Kabanda had hated Christians, but now he felt he had no choice. He must believe and ask this Jesus to restore his life. After all, his Islamic faith had not done much to help him.

After the prayer, the medics began to do their work of cleaning and dressing the wounds. Kabanda could see all the drips and equipment but still felt no pain, although he knew he was very weak. The realisation dawned on him that he was still on planet earth, where life had always been so hard for him and now was to get even harder!

As Kabanda seemed to be more fully conscious, Hugh began asking questions to find out who this young boy was and how to find his relatives. Kabanda was able to tell him and direct him to a nearby town where an uncle lived. This was the relative who lived closest to Kampala and the hospital.

Hugh went to look for the uncle even though it was still very wet and dark, and by God's grace he was able to locate him and bring him to the hospital. As Kabanda now had one of his own relatives with him, Hugh felt able to leave him.

By this time, it was very late, and Hugh had done all he could, so prayerfully and wearily he returned to the guest house where he was staying, leaving the boy in God's hands and his uncle's care.

Throughout the night, Kabanda was given bottle after bottle of blood tranfusions, and his uncle says he was extremely restless, but he remembers little of it. When morning came, he remembered that he had seen a white man by his bed. Was he a doctor? He asked the people who were around his bed, for by now his parents had arrived, as well as other relatives. They didn't seem to know who the mzungu was, or if they did, Kabanda's tortured brain was unable to retain the information.

He was tormented by endless thoughts rushing through his mind. He knew he was weak and had both an arm and a leg broken. How could he now do all his work of fetching and carrying? How could he now earn the money he needed to survive? Even his wonderful bicycle was now a tangled mass of metal.

As he lay there in bed, worries swirled around in his mind, and he felt his whole world had collapsed around him. He thought that perhaps it would have been better if he had died in the accident.

'Is there really someone called "God" out there?' Kabanda asked himself. 'If so, what have I done to be so punished, and why was I rescued? With all my problems, it would have been better if I had been allowed to die!'

In the middle of these wonderings, the doctors arrived and wanted to take Kabanda for an X-ray to make sure it was only the arm and leg that were broken and that they had not missed any other injuries. They required payment before they would carry out this procedure, but his parents did not have any money. Eventually an uncle found enough money for the procedure to be done.

At 8:00 a.m. the next morning, Hugh arrived with some friends to see how Kabanda was getting on. He met all the family, who were having a debate as to how they could pay for the medication and care that Kabanda needed.

Hugh was able to give the family the money needed for both the treatment and the hospital fees. That was such a huge relief to them, and they even managed to smile a little. With no welfare system, it is a huge burden for poor people to secure even the basic treatment that is needed if they become sick in Uganda, and without doubt Hugh's money was lifesaving for Kabanda.

The family were talking to Hugh, but as the pain and weakness increased, Kabanda was less and less able to look at the folk around his bedside. He wanted to communicate with Hugh, for he was still strangely aware of the peace that had come to him when Hugh had prayed over him the previous night. He wanted to tell him to keep on praying, especially since the pain was so bad in his chest.

Hugh and his friends had to leave and go to their commitments for the day, but Kabanda felt a great, intense urge to ask him something.

Somehow, he found the strength to focus and look at Hugh and with great effort was able to speak.

'Before you go, can you lead me in a prayer of confession? I want to learn to pray like you,' was Kabanda's request.

Hugh was taken by surprise at this sudden request from such a sick boy. Furthermore, all the relatives around his bed were wearing Islamic clothes, so clearly Kabanda had been brought up as a Muslim.

Hugh's face must have been a picture as he realised that God was at work in this boy's life. Here was someone who had hated the very mention of Jesus and to whom no one had ever preached the gospel, who was reaching out in faith before all his Islamic relatives, asking to accept Jesus into his life!

Hugh led Kabanda in a prayer of confession and commitment of his life to Jesus, and Kabanda knew in his heart that something amazing had happened, and peace came into his mind. Deep inside, Kabanda knew that Jesus would heal all his wounds, and he would walk again. With no previous teaching, he knew the hope and happiness which finding Jesus gives to a person. He knew that something real and life changing had happened inside him!

Hugh returned to visit Kabanda again that evening and continued to do so for the remaining ten days of his visit to Uganda. As he sat on Kabanda's bed, he began to tell him more about Jesus and the faith he had confessed.

The two grew close, and Hugh made a promise to Kabanda that he would be a father in God to him and always try to help him as much as was possible. He gave to Kabanda a Henderson family name, Nelson, which Kabanda cherishes to this day. Hugh also brought him a Bible and other Christian books so that in the long days and months ahead he could read, albeit slowly, and learn more about Jesus.

It was time for Hugh to return to Scotland, and he promised to visit his new son on the way to Entebbe airport to say goodbye. Aware that the days ahead would be very hard for this young lad, Hugh introduced him to a Ugandan pastor who promised to visit and encourage him from time to time.

Kabanda did not know the time of Hugh's flight and struggled to stay awake all day so that he would not miss him. At times it was impossible for him to keep his eyes open, and he slept. Each time he awoke, he was distraught in case Hugh had visited and he had missed saying goodbye! When it came to 5:30 p.m., Kabanda began to give up hope of seeing him and felt very sad.

His mother was by his bed and suddenly shook him. There was Hugh, standing at the bedside! It was a time of very mixed emotions as Kabanda was so pleased to see him but also so sad that he was now going back to his home. It was a difficult farewell for them both, but Hugh prayed with his son and left him with his UK address so that he could still be in contact with him.

6 Hospital days

Then followed a long period in hospital, where there was so little to encourage and much to discourage Kabanda. Anyone who has been hospitalised for a long time knows how slowly the days go by.

The doctors did their bed rounds at regular intervals and often had medical students with them. One such consultant always made comments like 'I doubt that his leg will ever join properly' each time he came.

His negative comments sank deep into Kabanda's mind. Although this consultant often related the story of the accident to the other medical staff he brought with him on the rounds, they did not look at the wound, dress it or give any medication. Without the mzungu's presence and authority and promise of payment, no one cared for Kabanda.

The lad was sad and missing his new father but also had the problem of almost no one caring for him in the hospital. However, there were occasional times when he did have a visitor. Hugh had an English friend who working in Uganda as a doctor, and he had asked him to keep an eye on Kabanda if he could. So from time to time, this young man Philip would stop by and see how Kabanda was progressing and send news back to Hugh. His visits were a lifeline to the boy and always brought much encouragement.

In Ugandan hospitals, a relative must stay with the patient and cook for them, and Kabanda's mother did this for the five months of his stay. It is sad that although she did this task, it was because it was her duty and not out of love. It could have been a time to build a relationship with her boy, but unfortunately, this did not happen.

On one of his visits, Philip brought a gift of £20 to help with the cost of food. As he was still bedbound and his mother had gone out to get drinks and to prepare food, Kabanda thought the safest place to keep the money was to stuff it down the plaster cast on his leg, which had a small 'window' where the medical staff could see the wound and clean it.

When Kabanda put the money in the cast, it disappeared right down into the leg, and he was unable to retrieve it. It was a huge blow to Kabanda to have lost such a large sum of money, but try as he could he was unable to pull the note out. In the end he gave up trying, and as time went by, he forgot all about it.

There it stayed for three months until the plaster was replaced in the theatre one day, and the doctor found the money. By now the note was beginning to change colour. No doubt it smelled too! What on earth was an English £20 note doing in the plaster?

When the doctor questioned him about it, Kabanda remembered how he had hidden it there. The doctor asked Kabanda to share the money with him. Because he was so happy that the money had been retrieved, Kabanda gladly agreed, and the doctor took care of having the £20 changed into Ugandan currency.

God moves in very mysterious ways, because from that time forward the doctor became his friend and began to take a special interest in Kabanda's leg and encouraged the other staff to look after him well and see he was treated properly. All of Kabanda's care improved, and his healing began to progress. Even the loss of the money had been part of God's way of caring for this boy!

After Kabanda had been in hospital for four months, it was decided to X-ray him again to see how the bones were aligning. The results of these X-rays showed that the arm had been broken from the shoulder and was not healing in a correct position.

It was a great disappointment, and the doctor felt it should be broken again and reset correctly. Such an operation would mean that Kabanda would have to stay in the hospital for another five to six months to receive treatment. His parents were asked to go home and think it over and come back with a decision the next morning.

Kabanda's family clan had a discussion and decided that they could not afford either the money or the time to stay with him in the hospital. The next morning when the theatre trolley arrived to take him for the operation, his parents refused to sign the consent form. The doctor was disappointed and warned Kabanda that he would never be very strong or able to do much physical work because his injuries were so profound, and his arm would always be in danger of breaking easily since it was in a wrong position.

After five months in Mulago Hospital, all the wounds except one had healed. The doctor friend now produced some crutches and helped Kabanda to stand and then begin to walk around the hospital ward.

It took a supreme effort even to stand after so many months in bed. Kabanda had not had physiotherapy to keep his muscles strong. However, it was so exciting for him to be able to feel his feet again and see he could stand with the help of crutches. Up until this time, even the medical staff had been very discouraging about him being able to walk again. Each day, for several minutes, morning and afternoon, Kabanda would try to stand. The effort to do this was enormous, and his body would become covered in sweat and he would be as out of breath as if he had just run a marathon!

When he tried to start walking, his doctor friend came to support and help him. He was told to be extremely careful and take it slowly in case he slipped and broke the leg again. This caution helped Kabanda to pace himself and be sensible, because his natural enthusiasm made him want to get going quickly! He did all the exercises faithfully, and his doctor friend gave up time each morning to assist him in walking around the ward and, gradually, from the ward into the corridor.

It was amazing how the Lord used that £20 gift far more than the donor could ever have anticipated. Kabanda's doctor friend had such a great influence in helping him heal and achieve a much better outcome from his injuries than might otherwise have been expected.

Finally, the day arrived when Kabanda could be discharged from the hospital, and he was carried outside to a taxi. He longed to just smell the fresh air outside but instead was bundled quickly into the taxi, because every minute meant money for the fare!

For Kabanda, the biggest challenge was now to be faced. It was not about being able to walk again or be strong enough to work but about being a young Christian going back to live in a Muslim village and home. God had been with him in the hospital; would he stay with him in the village?

7 Life back in the village

After five months in Mulago Hospital, it was such a contrast returning to village life. For the first week, Kabanda was something of a celebrity, and friends and relatives came to visit and see for themselves this boy who had survived such a horrendous accident and congratulated him on still being alive! Soon, however, the novelty of him being back in the village wore off, and life began to settle down again.

For Kabanda, the question of his new faith in Jesus Christ came under the scrutiny of his family. They were convinced he had made his declaration just to please the mzungu who had rescued him and paid for so much of his care. His parents could accept that it had been a reasonable decision, indeed it was very permissible to deceive this kind white man, but now that he was back at home, Kabanda could forget all that nonsense and return to the family faith of Islam. There was absolutely no need to continue with Christianity. To the family, it was a question of Kabanda just changing his mind; it had nothing to do with his heart.

As soon as Kabanda had mastered walking just a little without the aid of crutches, he set out to find if there was a local church to which he could go to learn more of his new-found faith. He found a church called the Sayuni Christian Church and was welcomed there and given support and fellowship as he shared his story.

In hospital, Hugh had given his adopted son a Bible, which became a very treasured possession and friend to Kabanda. As he read it, he found encouragement and began to understand a little more of his newly confessed faith. He also was learning more about prayer and spending time talking to his Saviour.

As Kabanda grew spiritually, so did the persecution from his family grow. They did all they could to discourage him and prevent him from going to church. The persecution grew into open hostility and then progressed to hatred.

One day, his father saw him and commented on the fact that he was looking unhappy. He knew his son was still far from strong and well. He called him over and asked him to look fully into his face and answer a question: 'My son, have you got saved forever, or just to please Mr Hugh?'

Kabanda did not know how to tell him the truth, that this was real and forever, but his father knew the answer just by looking at his son. He did not forbid his son to go to church as he might so well have done but allowed him to continue because of his own gratitude that the hospital bills had been paid by Hugh.

Kabanda's mother had no real insight as to what it meant to become a Christian, and she and other relatives in the home became increasingly violent in their treatment of Kabanda. This resulted in Kabanda leaning more and more on Jesus to help him in every way in his life. The prayer that was in Kabanda's heart was that the Lord would keep him faithful forever.

Although he was only a boy, he understood only too well how much opposition he would face from the Muslim community, especially since he was still a child in their eyes and officially under the authority of his parents and wider family. Family influence is very strong in

Uganda, and children are not brought up to be independent in the way that Western children are.

Within Kabanda was a growing desire to bring others to know the salvation he had experienced. When he had asked Jesus into his heart, something so real had happened that he could not and would not recant and just longed for others to experience this joy and peace in the same way.

In the village, Kabanda became increasingly isolated and rejected as he held to his Christian faith. He was often ignored by family and former friends. They could not understand the change which had happened in his life.

In spite of not having many friends to confide in, Kabanda continued to grow spiritually strong. His physical strength was returning too as he pressed on trying to walk with his crutches, even though he often had pain from the wound in his leg and badly healed arm. When people did come to talk to him, he would try to share his new faith with them, and some of his friends accepted Jesus as their Saviour and Lord.

The boy who had previously been his best friend in the village had no interest in becoming a Christian, and Kabanda was sad about that. As he prayed for him one day, he had an idea. Kabanda decided to write to Hugh and ask him to send a letter to this friend, because to receive a letter from a mzungu was a very prestigious thing. He did this, and Hugh wrote back a letter to Kabanda's friend.

The effect it had on the lad was dramatic: he instantly decided if this mzungu could be bothered to write to him, a 'nobody' in a remote village, then there must be something in this Christianity, so he decided to give his life to Jesus.

Chapter 7

Kabanda had no idea when he might see his new father Hugh again, but his new life in Christ had given him hope and purpose so that he was able to share the gospel not only by word but also by a changed life as well as the fact that he now had a good and helpful attitude towards others. These changes in behaviour gradually altered the way others treated him, and Kabanda was slowly winning their hearts.

When a great friend of his, called Stephen, asked to go to church with him one Sunday, Kabanda was filled with joy. At the end of the service, Stephen asked the pastor to say a prayer of salvation with him, and the joy knew no bounds! God had answered Kabanda's prayer for Stephen. Stephen was a popular boy who had many friends, and now these two young men began to share the gospel with them too.

All this time, Kabanda's leg was becoming stronger, and he was able to walk more and more without crutches and to attend more meetings in the church. This was helping him to understand better the faith he had embraced. He loved to read his Bible, to pray and to witness. He was finding fellowship and friendship with other believers. In these ways his life was becoming fulfilled and happy.

At home, things were not going so well. Kabanda's mother continued to persecute him. She had little love for her son and took every opportunity to tell him that his birth was an accident, for he should have been a girl. It was as if she blamed Kabanda for his gender and seemed to think he had tricked her with his birth by being a boy! The child who followed Kabanda was the longed-for daughter, and she continued to received special love and attention all the time.

This sister tried to help Kabanda by washing his clothes for him because his arm was so weak and painful. In fact, it was almost impossible for him to do his own washing, so he was very grateful for his sister's help. There were no washing machines to make the work light. Each article was scrubbed in cold water with a brush and a bar of soap or a sprinkling of soap powder! It was very hard work, even for a fit adult. When his mother found the girl doing this for her brother, she was so angry and forbade her ever to do it again! The whole village community was astonished at her hardness towards her son as she told him, 'You must wash your own clothes!'

In spite of the neighbours' disapproval, she continued to insist Kabanda do his own washing and other work. Life was hard as he painfully tried to do the chores expected of him. Even after all he had suffered, there seemed to be no love or even pity in her heart for him.

The Muslim leaders also hated Kabanda. Before the accident, he could be seen wearing Islamic clothes, carrying the Koran and attending the mosque every Friday, but now he was seen going to church every Sunday carrying his much-loved Bible.

The leaders constantly confronted his father and demanded that he forbid his son from attending the church, but his father was happy to allow his son to continue with his new faith. Kabanda's father even started writing letters to Hugh and boasted in the village that he now had an English brother! Even though he allowed Kabanda to continue, he didn't have the courage or desire to accompany his son to church because of his fear of the Muslim leaders, but he did continue to correspond with Hugh.

One day, Hugh's reply was a package. The package contained a lovely new brown Bible for Kabanda. As Kabanda opened the Bible in front of his father, to their amazement some money was hidden between the pages! His father was so surprised, recognising that it was money, but having no idea of English currency, he did not know the value. He didn't even know where to exchange it for Ugandan currency. He immediately stopped working and shut down his sewing machine, and the two of them caught the bus to Kampala.

Firstly, they went to the house of an uncle who lived in the city to show him this amazing gift. This uncle was more than happy to help Kabanda's father in exchanging the currency, and together they went to the forex bureau to do so.

The uncle did not have entirely pure motives, and seeing how totally inexperienced his relative was about the exchange rate, he cheated Kabanda's father, taking a good proportion for himself. Hugh had sent the money to pay for a whole year of schooling; but they only received enough for a term and a half.

The next morning, Kabanda and his father caught the bus back to Mukono and then walked the rest of the way to the village. When they arrived home, his father told Kabanda that he could prepare to return to school and continue his education from the point where he had been forced to stop because of the accident. What excitement! Kabanda had thought that his dreams of education had ended for good when the fish lorry had run him down all those months ago!

8 Back to school

I t was hard for Kabanda to really assimilate the truth that he was returning to school! He knew that God is the God of miracles and that with Him all things are possible, but when a miracle actually happens, it is hard to take in!

Kabanda's options were now extremely limited as he was disabled, but he went to the headmaster of the local secondary school, Trinity College, Mukono, and pleaded with him to be allowed to register. The headmaster was eventually persuaded to allow Kabanda to enter the school, especially since he had money in his hand to pay the fees in advance.

He enrolled in this new school with an enthusiasm to learn everything that was being taught and with a burning desire to share with his fellow pupils and friends about his faith in Jesus and how his whole life had been changed since he accepted Jesus to be his Saviour and Lord. Joy and hope were qualities of life that a person could really experience in their lives through faith in Jesus, and he wanted to share this good news!

Though it was a school with very poor academic standards, Kabanda tried as hard as he could to learn all that was being taught. Now that he no longer owned a bicycle or had to run errands all the time, there was a far greater opportunity to read and do homework. The money which had been sent by Hugh paid for a term, and Kabanda was able to reach the top of his class by working hard at his studies. Even though it was not a very good school, at least he was continuing his education.

Chapter 8

One day, walking to the school, he saw one of the most prominent Muslim leaders of the area. Kabanda pretended he had not seen him, for he knew the Muslims now hated him for changing faith, but the man called to him by name and so he had to answer. In Uganda it would be unforgivable to pretend you had not heard.

'Kabanda, I hear you have got saved. Is that true?' he asked.

God gave Kabanda the courage to reply. 'Yes, sir, it's true!'

The leader looked him straight in the eye. 'You are very stupid. I hate you,' was his answer.

It was not the first time that Kabanda had been insulted in this way since he had become a Christian, but it still hurt! He reminded himself that it was a joy to suffer for the name of Jesus, and he would have to face much humiliation in the days ahead.

Another joy he had was because he had been given the strength to answer truthfully when challenged, although he had been afraid. It would have been a hard thing for an adult to do, and Kabanda was still a boy.

The matter did not end there, because the same imam mobilised the Muslim community around his home village and organised a meeting. Before all the relatives and local community, Kabanda's father was called to answer why his son had disgraced them all and was shaming them. He was challenged as to why he did not stop his son from converting and was asked what he was going to do to bring him back to Islam.

Kabanda's father was unable to answer their charges, and since the whole community was already angry with him, he told them boldly that everyone in his family could have freedom of choice in the matter of faith and that he didn't mind if some of his children converted to Christianity because, after all, he had many children—there were plenty left to be good Muslims! It was really a remarkable answer from his father and showed the respect that he had for his son and his choice to become a Christian.

The hatred and persecution within the wider family continued, and although Kabanda was still a young Christian, he persevered in sharing with them all the love he had found in God. In later years, Kabanda heard and witnessed many testimonies of God's saving and healing power in the lives of others, but at this time he just shared what he had known in his own life. His father did not believe but was still supportive towards his son and did appreciate that being saved made a radical change to a life, that a person really did become a new person in Jesus.

Financially, the first year after the accident was extremely difficult. The months before Kabanda was able to go to back to school, his father had almost no money to support him, and Kabanda could do so little to help himself since he was still struggling to walk, mostly using crutches.

It also took about a year for the wound on the fractured leg to heal, and there was no treatment offered or available. Kabanda just kept praying and asking the Lord to heal it, because the wound was so bad that it seemed the leg could easily break again in that place. When he could, he tried to buy dressings and cover the wound himself, but he really needed antibiotics and good nursing care.

The persecution from the Muslim community continued, and many of his friends, as they realised this was a true change, declared their hatred for him and abandoned him. A 'good Muslim' would not associate with someone who had converted.

Kabanda's father kept up his correspondence with Hugh, and the replies were such an encouragement. In one letter, Hugh said, 'I look forward to seeing you when I come later in the year.'

When Kabanda heard this news, he was overjoyed! He tried to imagine what it would be like to see again the man who had taken pity on him when he had been left almost dead by the road and then had done so much for him.

Kabanda kept praying for Hugh as the days went by, asking that he would be brought back safely to Uganda. It was a little like a dream, for he could not really imagine that Hugh was coming again to Uganda. Perhaps he had meant something different in the letter and they had misread it?

That month of waiting seemed just endless! Finally, Kabanda went to Hugh's Ugandan colleagues at Lugazi to confirm if Hugh really was coming and that it was not something Kabanda had dreamt up. The excitement kept mounting within him, and he could hardly contain it.

Over the years since the accident, Kabanda had endeavoured to keep in contact with these pastors at the Lugazi church and visit them when possible. It was quite a long way to travel from his home village and not easy to do when you had crutches or difficulty in walking.

The pastors always welcomed him, prayed with him and encouraged him, teaching him more about the faith he had confessed as his own. Now they even arranged to take Kabanda to the airport at Entebbe so that he could be there to meet his benefactor and welcome him. That was beyond his wildest expectation!

Night after night, as the time approached, Kabanda would dream and try to imagine what it was going to be like to see Hugh again. When the great moment arrived, Hugh too was amazed to see his adopted son back on his feet and at the airport to welcome him, and he whisked him up in the air onto his shoulders, so thrilled that the Lord had answered his prayers! He had prayed that one day Kabanda would walk again, and now here he was at the airport to greet him!

Kabanda sat beside Hugh in the car as they made their way to Kampala, so excited to be with him. He couldn't understand much of what he was saying, because as yet he had learnt very little English, besides which Hugh spoke with a strong Scots accent. However, he was content to see the smiles and read in the body language that Hugh was happy to be back and with him. They developed a kind of 'smile language' between them! That trip also helped Kabanda to make a resolve to learn English.

Before Kabanda returned to his home, it was arranged for Hugh to make a visit to the family during his stay in Uganda, so Kabanda was even happier. He told his parents the news, and then he started to use the days before the visit to clean up the compound around the house and to plant flowers and grasses so that it would be beautiful to welcome his special guest. As the week progressed, so his excitement mounted. His Scottish Dad was coming to his home to see him!

The following Saturday, Hugh arrived for the visit. It caused quite a stir in the village. Everyone wanted to see this mzungu who would deign to visit such a poor village. He was welcomed with great honour, and a choir gathered at Kabanda's little house and sang songs for him.

The wider family had all come to the house, and they enjoyed the day as Hugh shared with them. Hugh had an invitation to preach to them, and it was an amazing opportunity. He had liberty to share with the village community the love of Jesus and how He died for them, and the people listened because they were so surprised that a white man would come and sit in a poor house and teach them. This visit made Kabanda's parents realise that the Christian faith was truly a source of love and happiness.

Evening came, and the visitors began to leave the house. Then Hugh was able to speak alone with Kabanda's parents and tell them that he wanted to continue to help with their son's school fees but that he would like him to attend a better school. His parents were happy to hear this and had no objection to any arrangement that Hugh might make.

So a few days later, he returned to the village and took Kabanda to the secondary school that was associated with the Lugazi church. They went shopping to buy the necessities that Kabanda was required to have, and he was admitted to this boarding school.

9 Lugazi school

Boarding schools in Uganda are for the children of the elite. Never in his wildest dreams had Kabanda ever thought that he or anyone else in his family would attend one! Not only are they more expensive than the day schools, but all the fees for the term must be paid in advance, and this is something very few families can do.

It was considered a miracle that Kabanda could go to boarding school, not only by his immediate family but also by the wider community of the village where he lived. Here was this small, poor boy being admitted to a boarding school, and all the fees for the entire year had been paid.

As much as his injured leg would allow, Kabanda danced and leapt for joy! He certainly praised God and thanked him for this British parent who had taken on the responsibility for his education.

Before Hugh left Uganda, he asked one of the pastoral team at Lugazi to be the guardian of Kabanda and to act as a link. This man was entrusted with the fees to pay for the schooling as well as for any medical fees in case of sickness and other expenses that Kabanda might need for books or equipment. It seemed to be a good arrangement, and Hugh felt he had left his son in good hands at the end of his visit to Uganda but, sadly, time was to show it wasn't as good as he had hoped.

One week after Hugh's departure, the term started, and Kabanda was the first pupil to join the class, with all the fees paid, ready to begin his studies. Sometimes it all seemed like a dream to the boy, because it was just so improbable that he should be at a boarding school.

The first big hurdle to face was language! Up until this time, Kabanda had experienced a very interrupted education, repeatedly being sent home from school because there was no money to pay fees and waiting months before he could return. All the previous schools he had attended had been of a very low standard, so the English taught was extremely rudimentary. Now he had to cope with all the classes being in English and most of the pupils already being fluent.

Before he left the country, Hugh had introduced Kabanda to a teacher whose speciality was the English language. She began to give Kabanda some private tuition so that he could catch up with the other students and cope more easily in class.

These lessons were an enormous help, for adjusting to the new life in a boarding school in itself was difficult without the extra problems of language. His parents were far away and unable to visit, so it was lonely for Kabanda until he had gained enough English to be able to converse with his fellow classmates and make friends with them.

Life in an African boarding school is a different experience from attending one in the developed world. There are no kindly matrons or houseparents to oversee the welfare of the children, who are left to fend for themselves. Life at Lugazi High School was particularly tough and a steep learning curve for Kabanda.

The dormitory was an old house by the school which had previously been the home of the headmaster. It was very cramped and had triple bunk beds for the boys to sleep in. The pastor who was given guardianship of Kabanda bought a mattress for him, but although he had been given money for a blanket, he told Kabanda that he didn't need one, neither sheets.

When he arrived at the dormitory, Kabanda found all the lower bunks already occupied and only a top one remaining. There was no way that Kabanda could climb up to reach his bed, so he had to plead with the boys, asking one of them to change with him. It was not a good start! Eventually one boy did agree, and Kabanda was able to have a bottom bunk. All the other boys had sheets for their beds, but Kabanda had to lie on the bare mattress. In the rainy season it can be quite cold at night, but he had to manage the best he could.

The school day began at 6:00 a.m., when the boys were woken up to do an hour's prep. After this, they went back to the dormitory to get washed and dressed in school uniform, ready for the first lesson, which began at 7:30 a.m.

Break time didn't come until 11:00 a.m., by which time everyone was starving! During the twenty-minute break, they were provided with a cup of thin porridge made from maize flour. The boys were supposed to provide their own sugar to sprinkle on it and make it a bit more palatable. The content of this breakfast never changed. It was the same day in, day out, year after year. The boys and girls grumbled to each other but were so hungry they had no choice but to eat it.

After this, lessons recommenced and continued until 1:30 p.m., when it was lunchtime. The food was awful! The meals consisted of a very poor quality maize flour which was made into a slightly thicker gruel called 'posho'.

There was no dining hall. The pupils just made their way to the kitchen area and lined up for their serving, then took it to the dormitory for eating. It was the same menu every day of the year,

Chapter 9

excepting Easter Sunday when the diet was supplemented by a little beef. Often the posho was badly cooked and almost inedible.

The distance from the kitchen to the dormitory was about half a kilometre, and alongside the path ran a wall. This wall became a way for the students to alert each other about the condition of the posho! The first person to get his portion would take a piece and throw it against the wall. If it stuck to the wall, it was deemed inedible! If the other pupils saw the posho stuck on the wall, they knew it was not worth queuing up any longer! Often, they returned to the dorm and only had a drink of water.

The same secret communication applied for supper, although beans would be served with this portion of posho. The school was not providing adequate food at all, and many of the parents knew this so, on visiting days, they took food parcels to their children.

The academic standard, however, was good, so some parents put up with the bad housekeeping and supplemented it instead. They also were often generous with pocket money so that their offspring could go out and buy good things to eat, but of course for Kabanda, there was no one at hand to take him out, treat him to extra food or give him pocket money. He learned to live with hunger as his constant companion.

He soon used the pocket money Hugh had left with him, and on school visiting days his parents were unable to come. Even the pastor who had been appointed as guardian was beset with severe personal problems so that he did not come to the aid of Kabanda.

Once again, life was very difficult, and Kabanda had no way whereby he could communicate the situation to Hugh and tell him about it. After a short time, the guardian stopped enquiring after Kabanda's well-being. It seemed as if Kabanda's parents had also given up responsibility for him now that he was at boarding school.

The weekend at school was boring, particularly for Kabanda since he was still quite crippled. Saturday morning started as usual with lessons until 10:00 a.m., after which they had breakfast.

Afterward it was time to wash their clothes. Again, it was a real problem for him to manage this as his arm was weak and painful. He tried as best he could but sometimes in desperation would beg one of his friends to help him. He even traded his precious ration of sugar for help. At times even this was to no avail, for if the parents had visited and the students were stocked up with supplies, they did not need his sugar! After these washing sessions, Kabanda's arm would be so painful that he was not able to write and do his homework.

On Saturday afternoons, there were sports like volleyball, basketball and football. It was so frustrating for Kabanda to have to stay on the sidelines and cheer his friends on when he so wanted to take part, especially in football.

One afternoon, in inter-class competitions, he watched his class as they were defeated by a much younger year group and felt humiliated for them. He then decided he was going to begin to train and play again. Before the accident, he had loved to play in the position of fullback defender and was good at football.

The training paid off, and Kabanda began to regain his old skills, so much so that he was invited to join his class team. Some of the teachers were very apprehensive, but he managed to persuade them that he was fit enough to play.

His classmates were really pleased to see him taking part because they had witnessed all his physical problems resulting from the accident. The first game in which he played was a great success, and their team won 2–1. Kabanda was so happy, and for the whole week which followed, he was excited. He was so looking forward to the following Saturday when he could play again.

Somehow, the news of the football match had reached the pastor who was acting as guardian to Kabanda, and he became angry.

'If you play football and get injured, then I will have to spend all the money for your upkeep on getting you better,' he yelled at the boy. 'I forbid you to play!'

'I must run around and get exercise,' answered Kabanda, 'but I promise I will not play in any important match.'

However, the following term there was a big interschools' competition, and the other pupils kept approaching Kabanda and begging him to join the team and help them. They felt that they could not possibly win unless he was one of the defenders on their team. He didn't really need too much persuading; he loved the game so much he agreed to accept his usual role of fullback defender.

The match began and was going well, and Kabanda was really enjoying the thrill of it all when one of the other side fouled him, kicking his right leg just where it had been fractured so badly.

It was disaster! Kabanda was down on the ground and rolling around in absolute agony. He was carried from the pitch to a clinic for treatment. The injury was so bad that he needed to miss school for the next two weeks. Today, Kabanda admits to telling his friends and teachers that if they saw his guardian looking for him to tell him that Kabanda was very busy preparing for exams!

10 Dark days

The long-term malnutrition that Kabanda was experiencing began to affect the healing of the wound on his leg, and although two years had now elapsed since the accident, the wound had not healed but rather was deepening. It would seem to heal over a little but then break down into an open wound again.

The pain was dreadful to bear, and Kabanda began to be depressed and feel that life was no longer worth living. He felt his leg was just going to rot away and break off. The wound was infected and had a vile odour, and all he had was a small bottle of iodine as well as peroxide with which he could bathe it. He had bought these medicines from a pharmacy and had no instruction on how to use them, but he used them to try and clean up the infected wound.

Eventually the leg became so bad that he decided he would have to get himself back to Mulago Hospital, which was miles away in the capital, Kampala, where he had been initially treated. It was a problem to get some transport all the way to Kampala. After a while, Kabanda managed to get enough money together for the bus fare and arrived at the hospital, only to find long queues of people waiting to be seen.

But he had come this far and was not going to be defeated! Eventually he did manage to get the leg looked at by a doctor, who asked him to return in one week. Kabanda felt a little more hopeful that he might get well, but when the time came for his second appointment, he could find no way to get more money for transport back to Mulago

Hospital, and there was no one to help him, so he had to miss the appointment at the clinic.

The situation became so bad that his leg would no longer support him, and walking became impossible. Eventually he shared his plight with a school friend, and she mentioned it to her mother. On the next school visiting day, this lady came to see Kabanda and asked to look at his wounded leg. When she saw the wound, she was horrified and was sure Kabanda would need to have the leg amputated, so she gave him money to return immediately to the hospital.

Glad to have help, Kabanda left Lugazi the next morning before light and arrived early at the hospital. Even with his prompt start, there was already an extremely long queue to see the doctor.

When he eventually did see the doctor, the consultant refused to treat him because his parents were not with him and he was still under age. Furthermore, only patients who had money at hand were treated. Kabanda had neither money nor adults with him. He was told by the medical staff that he needed another operation on his leg and to return when he could pay for it.

Now what was he to do? There seemed only one way forward—to go back to his village. Kabanda went home to his parents and told them be needed another operation, but they had no money to help him.

After meeting this negative response, Kabanda went back to Lugazi to seek out the pastor who was supposed to be his guardian. It took several days to locate him, and when he did it was just to be met with disappointment again, for the pastor was unable or unwilling to help.

The boy felt abandoned. These were dark days when everything was a struggle.

Kabanda was now left without anyone to help, and he was convinced that his leg would drop off. It seemed to him that the infection was eating all the bone away. The pain was excruciating too, and he had no way of relieving it. He didn't even have enough money to buy an aspirin.

Other problems were also besetting him, for he had run out of pens and exercise books for his lessons. Even though he enjoyed his classes and his English was improving, not having simple things like writing materials was a real problem.

Kabanda had one aim during this time. He wanted to learn English so that when his father Hugh came back from Scotland, Kabanda would be able to talk to him fluently and explain his problems! To this end he worked as hard as he could.

He was also trying to improve his overall academic position in the class. He had gone into Senior Three, which was the equivalent of the British O Level. By the end of the first term, he had managed to reach ninetieth place out of ninety-six students. Despite this low ranking, he was both surprised and happy to have attained it since he had such poor English and was determined to get higher up the ladder!

Kabanda worked hard. He recalls he was the only pupil without a school uniform, books and so many other things. The headteacher was the only person who accepted that he had a reason for these problems and didn't chase him out of the class. He knew Hugh had paid the fees but was far away. As far as Hugh knew, the money he left and sent was being used to help Kabanda. He had no idea that it wasn't reaching him.

In the second term of the school year, Kabanda became extremely sick. The poor nutrition, the infected leg and the general deprivation had caught up with him. He developed a fever with a cough and was bringing up fresh blood. He had no idea what to do; it seemed to him as if the whole world had abandoned him.

He was still only a teenager! For a few days, he felt too ill to leave the dormitory and go to lessons, so he stayed in bed.

No one came to check what had happened to Kabanda. As soon as he could, he tried to get back to class, because he did not want to fall behind in his grades. He dragged himself out of bed and managed to reach the classroom, only to collapse in the doorway.

Then he was taken by someone to the school dispensary. This was just a building without medical staff or any medication, but he was allowed to stay there on a bed until he had regained enough strength to start looking for some help.

Once again, Kabanda went in search of the pastor who had been designated as his guardian. This time he was more successful and managed to locate him. The guardian promised he would come and take him to the nearest hospital, so Kabanda went back to school to wait for him, but sadly he didn't keep his word.

When Kabanda realised he was not going to have help, he decided the only thing he could do was to somehow travel back to his home. He could not get to classes in school and could not take care of himself. He had no alternative.

Somehow, Kabanda managed to make the journey home. All his life seemed to have collapsed around him.

When he arrived to the village, his parents were horrified to see their son looking like a skeleton, barely able to make it through their door. They knew he needed urgent treatment but were only able to afford the very poorest of local clinics, where they took him. Kabanda stayed in that shelter for three days, receiving no real medical help.

In his exhaustion and pain, all he could do was lie and rest. He ate a little food that his family provided. After three days, Kabanda felt that perhaps he now had enough strength to get back to school. He would have to fend for himself, for there was no one anywhere to help him, but at least at the school he had a bed to sleep on! To have a bed and a roof over his head was his priority.

As he made his way through the school gates, Kabanda was besieged by some of his friends from whom he had borrowed small amounts of money so that he could get transport to his village in order to recover. Seeing him come back, they thought he must have come to return their money, and he had such trouble trying to convince them that he had none.

Kabanda felt terrible that he had needed to borrow money from school friends in the first place and now was so miserable because he was totally unable to pay them back. Most of the pupils in the school came from homes where their parents had enough money to provide all the basic needs, so they did not understand the terrible situation in which Kabanda now found himself.

Although things seemed very dark and at times the problems almost insurmountable, Kabanda still had an awareness that God had a plan for his life. This helped him to persist in his studies despite the physical disabilities and lack of financial support. God had rescued him from both physical and then spiritual death and allowed him to get to this school.

Even so, it was a dark time spiritually and a struggle to hold on to the Lord. It was hard to pray; it seemed as if the prayers only went to the ceiling and bounced back. It was hard to sing or try to praise God. He knew God was there, somewhere, but where were the answers to promises of provision and care? It seemed as if his Muslim relatives would have reason to mock him now. It had been relatively easy to testify to them that he had a wonderful heavenly Father when all was going well, but it was a very different story now he was going through such bad times. It seemed as if no one drew near to encourage or strengthen Kabanda through this dark time. He almost despaired of living, and perhaps he would have done so had he not been able to make progress with his studies.

The teacher of English, who was called Nancy, did prove to be a friend in continuing to help with the language, especially with conversation. Out of school hours, while others played, Kabanda would tune in to the BBC World Service so that he could learn by listening to the language.

All this helped him to improve academically, especially in the English class. Indeed, Kabanda only spoke to other students in English, even if they were speaking in the vernacular, because of his aim to be fluent the next time he saw Hugh.

By the end of the second term at Lugazi, despite all the sickness, Kabanda had attained third place in the class, and finally, at the end of the third term, he reached the top! This was a reflection of his aptitude and also attitude, a remarkable achievement for a boy with such an unpromising background and who was so unwell.

It meant that Kabanda was promoted into Senior Four for the next school year and could prepare to sit the O Level and national exams at the end of it.

11 Senior Four

The hard work of the previous school year had brought Kabanda to the notice of and given him favour with his teachers, so the new term started promisingly. Kabanda also experienced God intervening in his life in a remarkable way, bringing him healing. Up until this time, he had been in so much pain, and there was still an open wound in his leg.

One evening, he was taking a bath in the wash house, and he noticed something white coming out of the open place in his leg. He was terrified and was sure his leg was now going to fall off as he had so often feared! He sat down on the cold, wet, concrete floor and decided he had nothing to lose in pulling this thing out, and as he did so, he realised it was a piece of bone.

It was not easy and it hurt to pull it, but he couldn't stay with it sticking half out! His fear and pain made him feel sick inside. His worst fear was that once the bone had been removed, he would never be able to stand again!

Finally, quite a large piece of bone was in his hand; it presumably had been broken off during the accident. Very fearfully, Kabanda put his hand on the wall and tried to get up, still very worried that his leg was going to somehow detach itself and fall off. He felt so alone and so ill, but he could not stay forever in the washroom with a piece of bone in his hand, so he slowly stood up and put weight on the leg.

It didn't fall off! He discovered he was able to stand. Shaking all over and in a cold sweat, he wrapped a towel around his naked body, left all his washing gear and clothes in the wash house and walked very gingerly over to the dormitory.

Somehow, he couldn't believe he was actually walking; he still thought at any moment the leg might drop off, the one fear that had been his constant companion for years. Was this real? Was it some sort of dream? Slowly, Kabanda entered the dormitory and laid himself down on his bed. He promptly fell into a deep sleep.

When he woke up, it was time for study. He thought about what he should do and decided to miss the evening preparation class, afraid that if he went, someone might knock his leg and it would fall off.He closed his eyes and fell back into a deep sleep. He slept and slept, and when he awoke, he knew he had been touched by God in healing.

It was not something he could have explained to anyone, but deep in his spirit he knew that God had touched his leg; he just knew he had experienced a miracle of healing. Three days later, the wound had closed over and dried up! The severe scarring remains to this day, but the wound was healed.

12 Derek's visit

In 1999, Kabanda was entering Senior Five and preparing to take the O Level and government exams. By this time, Hugh had changed ministry from working for The Gate church in Dundee to working for an interdenominational mission charity, so it was a friend and colleague of his called Derek who led a team from Dundee to Uganda in 1999. Kabanda had met Derek from time to time when Derek and Hugh had travelled together in Uganda.

Derek planned to visit the community and school at Lugazi. He wanted to help Kabanda since Hugh was not able to visit that year, and he contacted Kabanda before his trip and asked him if there were any items which he needed.

Things he needed? The list would have been endless if Kabanda had written everything down. He made a list of the things he most needed for the coming school year and sent them off to Derek, hardly daring to hope that he might bring them. Many of the things on the list Derek was able to carry with him from Scotland, including a lovely pair of leather shoes that fitted perfectly. Kabanda was so proud of those shoes and took great care of them.

The headmaster of the school gave Derek a report on Kabanda's excellent progress and told him what an asset he was in school because of his hard work, academic excellence and good attitude. He encouraged Derek to help provide the practical things which were needed each year so that Kabanda could continue with his schoolwork.

The result of this talk was that Derek suggested a trip to a supermarket in Kampala. This was a great adventure for Kabanda. They went to the city, and as they walked up and down the aisles, Kabanda was invited to pick out stationery, school uniform clothes and even a blanket that he needed. He was told to choose whatever he required for school. It was like many Christmases and birthdays rolled into one!

'The son of a mzungu should have all he needs!' was Derek's comment. It wasn't right that a white man's son should starve. It had shocked Derek to see how thin Kabanda was.

During the time they spent together, Kabanda was able to really share with Derek the things that had happened to him throughout the school year after Derek and Hugh had gone home following their last visit. It was such a relief to Kabanda to be able to unburden his heart and tell someone of all the privations and difficulties he had encountered. Derek's visit had become the light at the end of a very long, dark tunnel, bringing hope and a feeling of humanity again to Kabanda. To know that someone understood how hard it had been and who cared and was in a position to help was amazing.

To be able to be like everyone else and have clothes, books, even a blanket on his mattress—he felt like the son of a king! It was easier to praise God, for his heart sang with joy for his healed leg and all the wonderful gifts. Coming from being totally locked into poverty, he now had the essentials for living at school.

Before he left, Derek commented, 'I expect to hear even better grades next time!' and gave Kabanda a gift of money to buy textbooks for the national exams so that he could perform to the very best of his ability.

Kabanda was overwhelmed by the love and generosity shown to

him. He thought about the money he had been given and reflected on his experience of hardship through the last school year. He decided to buy only the most essential textbook and to bank the rest of the money as a nest egg in case of future needs. He went to the headmaster and confided in him and with his help was able to set up a bank account.

He knew the headmaster was a man he could trust. By this stage in his school career, he had established a good relationship with the headmaster and also with some of the other teachers because they admired his serious attitude to learning. Soon he found these teachers were more than willing to help him by loaning him various textbooks from time to time to help him with his coursework. This meant he did not have to spend so much money buying books and had a little more for food and writing materials.

All the hard work and perseverance through the years brought its reward, which was a 1st class grade in the national examination that year! It had been a hard struggle, but it had all been worth it, and the school was proud of Kabanda.

These examinations were followed by a very long eight-month holiday, so Kabanda needed to find a home for that time. He went back to his home village but was not able to stay in his parents' house since it was so small and the family had grown to fifteen children. Kabanda was one of ten boys.

He decided to ask one of his older brothers if he could stay with him, for this brother had settled in a nearby small town, and Kabanda hoped to be able to find some work there through the holiday. One would have hoped that Kabanda's family would have been proud of this young man, but instead there was a lot of jealousy directed towards him from his siblings because he was now an educated man.

Chapter 12

None of Kabanda's brothers had been educated beyond primary school level, and although they now had some paid work, all of them refused to house or help feed him. The old animosity was still there, as well as the anger at his abandoning Islam and becoming a Christian. Within the family, there was no forgiveness or compassion offered.

Eventually, Kabanda found somewhere to live in that hostile community. He found casual labour when he was able, but even that was hard to get. It was not easy to get employment in Uganda, and when jobs became available, they were often given to relatives rather than being fairly advertised.

The song 'God will find a way, where there seems to be no way' was an encouragement to Kabanda through these months. He did not know what his future held, for although he had done so well in his school examinations, he had no knowledge of whether Hugh or Derek could help support him through the next two years of higher education that would lead into university entrance. He really wanted to go back to school for the next two years.

One thing Kabanda learnt to do through that long vacation was to use a fax machine, and he began to communicate with his sponsors in this way. One Saturday morning, he received a fax from Derek which asked him, 'Do you want to continue to a higher level of education?'

Derek indicated that he and Hugh were willing to continue with financial support. This was such a wonderful answer to Kabanda's prayers. God had found a way where there seemed to be no way!

Kabanda wanted to fax straight back 'Yes!' but had no money in his pocket to do that. He went home very happy and looked for some more work to get enough money to send his reply, for he so longed to continue with his education.

13 The last years of school

A t the end of the eight months of vacation, Kabanda packed
his few things in a bag and returned to school to enter what
in the British system is known as sixth form college. The
school staff were thrilled to welcome him back, because they could
see this boy had great potential and he maybe would make such good
grades that he would put their school on the map in terms of Uganda's
educational system!

Even Kabanda's very attitude to work was a good example and
encouragement to other pupils. He began to organise debating
societies within the school, which helped learning outcomes for
students. Leadership qualities that had been forged in the fires of
persecution and hardship were beginning to emerge in Kabanda.
This boy had survived and overcome so many challenges through his
teenage years that they were now producing a harvest.

Hugh wrote to him during that year to tell him that he was coming
back to Uganda with his new ministry, not to Lugazi but to a place
called Ggaba on the shores of Lake Victoria. Hugh, of course, had kept
in close contact and knew all about his son's academic success.

Kabanda was longing to see Hugh and talk with him again. The
date drew near for his proposed visit, and Kabanda went to see the
headmaster to ask permission to go to Ggaba and visit Hugh. The
headmaster agreed without any hesitation, but Kabanda also felt
morally bound to ask his 'guardian'. The pastor refused permission

and said he would go himself and see Hugh on behalf of Kabanda so that there would be no need for him to miss school.

Disappointed by his guardian's answer, Kabanda tried to accept it, but the desire to see his Dad Hugh was so great, it burned within him. He had no idea how long Hugh was proposing to stay in Uganda, and so, after much thought and prayer, he decided to ignore the pastor's answer and go. It was not an easy decision for Kabanda because he was used to being unquestionably obedient to anyone in authority.

He made his way to Ggaba but had no idea where the guesthouse where Dad Hugh was staying was situated. After many enquiries, he found the office of the charity Hugh was working with, and from there he was directed to the guesthouse. He tried to follow the directions, but they were not very clear, and he became lost. Eventually he found someone who knew exactly where it was and was willing to take him there.

It was lunchtime when Kabanda arrived at the house where Hugh and the mission team were staying. As he entered the gate, two men came out of the building to see who it was they had spotted coming into the compound. One was Hugh, but the other was the pastor from Lugazi who was supposed to be Kabanda's guardian and who had forbidden him to come!

Kabanda felt himself freezing with fear and shock since he had disobeyed his guardian, but he also felt such a joy to see Hugh. For a moment he stood there, with these two emotions fighting within him, not knowing what to do, and then Hugh ran towards him to welcome him and hug him, while the pastor watched from a distance.

Although he had such a warm welcome from Hugh, Kabanda was still quite nervous as he went into the guesthouse and was introduced to the other members of the mission team. He could feel the disapproval of the pastor who should have looked after him through the years. Perhaps the pastor was afraid that Kabanda would tell tales on him and the truth would emerge about his lack of care and questions would be asked about the money that had been given for Kabanda.

Revenge was the last thing on Kabanda's mind; he just wanted to see his Dad Hugh! Yes, in time the truth was all told, but that was not what Kabanda wanted now. He wanted a hug! He just wanted to be in Hugh's company, and now that he was fluent in English, to be able to talk to him.

The rest of the day was spent in the guesthouse catching up with Hugh, and Kabanda was able to tell him a little of what life had really been like through the past few years. As Hugh questioned his son, Kabanda told him about the school results but also about the hunger and deprivation.

The pastor who was supposed to have acted as guardian had not wanted Kabanda to go and visit his mzungu father with good reason, because Hugh confirmed that he had been sending support all the time, and yet it had not been reaching his son. Those terrible years of hardship should never have happened. Yet they had and, sad though it was, God had used them in the life of this boy to make him stronger.

One of the things Hugh did as a result of the revelations of this visit was to give Kabanda a mobile phone so that in a real emergency he could always reach his father, even in Scotland. Although it was expensive to buy credit for the phone, it was still a lifeline. From that time onwards, Kabanda would be able to speak to Hugh in person should he need to get in touch.

Hugh was justly proud of all his son had achieved and encouraged him to continue working hard at school and to keep trusting the Lord and learning more about his love.

That evening, Kabanda returned to school with a phone, some pocket money and school supplies but with even more determination to excel in his studies and to follow the Lord with all his heart. It had been so right to have taken the day out of school and gone to meet his adopted father because he felt inspired and encouraged and strengthened to continue. There was such joy in his heart and so much thankfulness for the love and care he had received.

Throughout the two years of study for university entrance, Kabanda worked incredibly hard and maintained his position as top of the class. The big question was, 'Is top of the class in this school enough to gain a government sponsorship to university?'

Around this time, Derek had also returned to Lugazi and had indicated that neither he nor Hugh would be able to sponsor Kabanda through university. It was just too much money for them to raise as it was much more expensive than school fees.

There was only one possibility for Kabanda to enter university. The Ugandan government gave a few university scholarships to very bright pupils who excelled in their higher national exams. No one from Lugazi had ever gained such a scholarship, and was the standard in that school high enough for any pupil to gain one? It was certainly doubtful. The scholarships were few and far between and very hard to win.

Kabanda knew it was the only hope, however slim, of him ever getting to university, so he studied every spare minute of the day and night, praying and trusting the Lord to bless him. If effort was needed, then he would give 200% !

Derek's visit was just three months before the national finals, and once again, he took Kabanda out and bought him all the things he needed to see him through. That was such a help. Kabanda needed lots of paper and pens to take notes, not just in lessons but also from the books he borrowed from his teachers. There was no library either in school or town where he could browse, nor computers where he could access information online.

Derek tried to encourage Kabanda with the thought that even should he fail to get to university, he had achieved far more than any of his family, and he had managed to do this even with the disabilities of both leg and arm injuries. Derek felt he should prepare Kabanda for the fact that it was so unlikely that he would win a scholarship that he would need to be able to carry on with his life regardless of what would happen.

There was also another problem which had been making life harder and harder for Kabanda. The injuries from the accident had left him with a great weakness in his right arm, making writing for any length of time very painful. Writing examination papers was a great ordeal and only achieved by dosing himself with considerable amounts of paracetamol.

Kabanda had done so well, and everyone was exceptionally proud of him, but it was doubtful that he would be able to write for the hours that were required for the final year national exams. It was almost a physical impossibility, even if he had the academic knowledge to write the papers.

Derek's talk with him only served to make Kabanda even more determined that he would go to university. He had come this far, and by the grace of God he would go further. Something deep within him spurred him on, and he could not accept the fact that he might just have to go home to his village when the school year ended.

The school administration had made a promise that the pupil who came top in the mock examinations would have their last term's fees paid for them as a prize. Such a challenge inspired Kabanda so that once again he came top of his class, winning this prize. He was able to tell his guardian that he did not need his fees paid for the final term.

The results of the mocks were also an encouragement as they were set externally rather than by the Lugazi school teachers. This meant that he was up to standard and well on the way to achieving a scholarship level.

The scripture that was such an encouragement to Kabanda at this time was Jeremiah 29:11: '"For I know the plans I have for you," declares the Lord, "plans to prosper you and not to harm you, plans to give you hope and a future."'

God must have a future for him! He had rescued him, saved him from physical and spiritual death, preserved him through so many setbacks. Kabanda knew that God had a plan for his life that was good and would give him a hope and a future.

In his heart, he determined to get closer and closer to the Lord, and to know and serve him was his deepest desire, whatever happened about university. God has used this part of his word to speak to many, many of his children through the centuries, and certainly it was a word to this young Ugandan boy at this time in his life.

14 The big temptation

We all know how the pressure mounts at the end of the school year when important examinations loom large, and this was certainly the case for Kabanda and his fellow students as they approached the final external exams that could lead them to university entrance.

At Lugazi school, very few of the students came from families who could afford to send their children to university, so the only hope for them was to try to win a government sponsorship. These were few and far between, and the school at Lugazi had never yet managed to have a pupil attain one. The students who won them usually came from schools with very high academic records and to which the children of Uganda's elite were sent. Although Lugazi was far better than the village secondary schools, it was not in the same league as these elite schools, so little hope was ever had that a pupil might get such a scholarship.

The days flew by as both the teachers and students worked hard to prepare for their examinations. Even without much hope of a scholarship, all the staff and pupils wanted the best results they could achieve in order that the students might be able to get jobs and maybe at a later date save enough money for the fees needed for university entry.

About a week before the exams were due to start, some strangers arrived at the school. They walked around the compound and talked to the senior students but kept out of the way of the staff. When they had identified the students who were doing the final exams, they introduced themselves as officials from the examination board and said they wanted to help them to pass. They then asked the young people for a sum of money, quite a large sum for the pupils to find, but in return they promised to get for them information which would help them to pass the exams. They promised they would find out what the questions would be so that the students could know and prepare in advance. It was a huge temptation to cheat, not just to get good grades but perhaps have the possibility of getting a coveted place in university!

'What we now need,' they explained, 'is a contact telephone number, so that when we have the information, we can pass it on.'

The only person in the school who had his own mobile phone was Kabanda. He was prevailed upon by his classmates to give his number to these 'officials', and the students paid the money required.

Up until this time, Kabanda had been praying, relying on the Lord who had got him this far to take him through the exams. Once he had allowed his phone number to be used in this way, he found his peace had vanished and he could no longer feel the presence of the Lord with him.

He was very miserable and, as the days went by, a battle raged within him. To pass the exams was the goal of so many years' hard work; his future career and life hung on it, yet he had sacrificed his integrity to try and make sure he did pass. It was a terrible time. His conscience bothered him day and night. He tossed and turned on his bed, and in daytime he found it hard to concentrate on revision. Each day seemed worse than the one before.

Two days before the exams were due to start, he could bear it no longer. His mind became full of thoughts of how faithful God had been to him, how the Lord had saved him in the accident and brought him to this place in his life. These thoughts were so overwhelming that Kabanda knew he could not go on and cheat in this way. Even if he were to fail the exams, it was better to be honourable rather than cheat!

In a country where corruption is so rife at every level, this was a brave decision to make. He knew he would lose the friendship of his classmates and even possibly have to cope with their anger, but he had to do what he knew was right.

On his knees in repentance, he asked the Lord to forgive him, whatever the cost or outcome of his decision to retract might be.

Then he had to face his fellow students and say they could not use his phone! It meant sabotaging the whole arrangement, and of course everyone had paid money to be part of this cheating scam. The students were furious with Kabanda and would not accept his decision.

There was only one thing to do: Kabanda had to disable his phone so that it could not receive messages, and then he gave it to someone outside the school premises to look after it until the exam time had passed. That way no one could steal his phone or intimidate him and make him change his mind.

It was hard to take the wrath and opposition of the other pupils. They were vicious in their accusations against Kabanda, saying it was because he had a better academic class performance and so wanted them to fail! To be accused of such a mean attitude hurt Kabanda very much. Somehow, his classmates managed to get hold of another phone and continued with the plan.

Chapter 14

Once Kabanda had made his decision and taken his stand, he felt better. It was such a relief to have peace again in his heart and to sleep easily at night! He knew that whether he passed or failed the exams, he had done what was right in God's eyes and that the Lord would look after him.

The night before the exams, the borrowed mobile phone duly rang in the dormitory. As arranged, the bogus officials read out the questions. The pupils were repeating out loud what was being said to them, and Kabanda made a decided effort to cover his ears and not even hear anything by accident, because he had promised the Lord he would not cheat at any cost. It was like the temptation was being thrown at him again because it was really hard to cover his ears for a long time.

The next day, the exams began. The pupils were sitting and waiting for the command, 'Now turn your papers over. You can begin!'

When Kabanda did, he read through the questions, and they were all dealing with topics he had revised and with which he felt confident. As he sat writing the paper, he found that he knew the answers to every question. When the exam was over and they all gathered outside, he found out that the questions read over the phone were not the right questions on the paper anyway! The students who had cheated had been tricked and were very disappointed and angry.

The problems which Kabanda encountered throughout the exams were not due to inability to answer questions but to his physical disability. Ever since the accident, writing had been a painful activity for Kabanda, and if he was unwell with a fever, it was almost impossible, as the fever weakened the hand even more. Derek had supplied Kabanda with some strong analgesics to take while he was writing the papers, though they usually made him feel very dizzy.

One afternoon in the middle of the exams, the pain in the hand was so bad that Kabanda took a dose of these pills to help him through. They were so powerful that he dropped off to sleep in the middle of writing the paper! His headmaster was invigilating and tried to wake him up and give him cold drinks so that he could get back to work. Somehow, he managed to finish all the papers, but it was a miracle that he did. He either had to cope with pain and inability to write or take analgesics and feel doped.

The completion of the final examinations marked the end of Kabanda's school career, whatever the outcome. There was a new life ahead of him, whether or not he would have a place in university.

It was time to go home again. The school years were behind him for ever. Already an incredible miracle had occurred in his life—the very fact that he had completed secondary school.

-

15 Another setback followed by joy

After leaving school, Kabanda went back to his home village. As before, there was no room for him to stay at his father's little house, so he went to the home of a brother, who had agreed to give him a roof over his head for the vacation time. He urgently needed to find some work to pay for his keep, and his father agreed that he could help with working on the sewing machine and doing some tailoring with him. However, the business was poor, and even with the two of them working together, it produced so little income that after working all day, there was often not enough money to buy food.

Nevertheless, they continued to work together in this way, doing the best they were able, until it all came to an abrupt halt. Kabanda's father had a motorbike that he was buying through a microfinance scheme on hire purchase. It was his pride and joy, although it would probably take him the rest of his life to pay off the loan.

'I really need these clothes to be delivered quickly to a customer,' he said one morning to Kabanda. 'Can you go on the motorbike and deliver them, my son?'

'Of course,' agreed Kabanda. 'I'd love to do that.'

So Kabanda packed up the clothes into a package and set off. He had no crash helmet or other protective clothing to wear. The Ugandan roads are fine red dust, and as he set off, the air behind him was filled with clouds of it. He was enjoying the ride and well on his way when suddenly another vehicle collided with him. In seconds, he was lying injured on the road.

How could God let such a thing happen to him again? He lay hurt and bewildered, and very worried about his father's motorbike.

Bush telegraph is very swift, and soon someone had reached Kabanda's village and told his parents the news, and they were sure that this time it was the end for their boy. Surely, he could not survive two accidents, and if he did, then he would never be able to walk again.

Although his first thoughts were for the welfare of his boy, Kabanda's father also now had a terrible worry because he owed money on the motorcycle that he had no way of repaying. Without Kabanda at his side, the business would not do so well, and without the transport, he could not deliver as easily as before. And now maybe he also had a crippled son to support! These thoughts were spinning in his head.

Once again, Kabanda found himself on a hospital bed. His head ached, and his great worry was for his father, for he knew he was so poor and now had no motorbike, nor money to repay the loan.

The family and friends who gathered around his bedside confused him as he lay frightened and injured. He heard them as they spoke together about him. Some of the family now prophesied that he would certainly die in a third accident. Others declared that his ancestral spirits were angry with him, while still others just said he was useless and had no riding skills, so he had better keep away from all such forms of transport. All these comments brought emotional pain on top of the physical pain he was experiencing.

He lay there, traumatised and fearful. Surely God wouldn't abandon him now! God's honour was at stake, for his faith was firmly in the Lord, not the ancestral spirits or Mohammed.

After all the years of struggle at school, what was to happen to him now? Fortunately, Kabanda's injuries were not as serious as they first appeared, and they soon healed so that he was discharged from the hospital after about a week. He went back to the village, and as his strength returned, so did his confidence in the Lord.

In his spirit, he realised that God did indeed have his hand on his life and had protected him yet again from what could have been a fatal accident. Fatalities from road traffic accidents are common in Uganda, especially as so few people wear crash helmets when riding motorbikes and the highway code is constantly ignored.

Instead of the accident being a discouragement, it became an encouragement to Kabanda, and that in turn was a cause of wonder to the people around him. That he could still praise his God through it all was a clear testimony to them.

Once he was fully recovered, Kabanda resumed working and saved as much as he could, preparing in faith for university. He managed to buy a pair of shoes and put them aside so that he would look smart.

After work one evening, sitting in his brother's house, he heard the news on the radio. It was announced that the results of the national examinations were published, and students were instructed to return to their schools and collect them.

What a mixture of emotions flooded Kabanda's heart. Sleep completely evaded him that night as he stirred with excitement yet with a tremendous fear of possible failure filling him. Could he have passed? What if he had failed? What if he had won a scholarship? No, that would really be an impossibility for someone from the Lugazi school! His mind flitted from one thought to another all through the night.

His father called by the house the next morning because he too had listened to the radio. He brought with him a gift for Kabanda. It was a little money to pay for transport back to school. It was such a sacrificial gift.

Kabanda felt that first he should telephone the headmaster and find out the results that way because if he had not done well, it would save the expense of a trip to Lugazi. As the phone was ringing, Kabanda's heart was beating as loudly as the ringing tone.

'Congratulations, Kabanda!' were the amazing words he heard. He couldn't believe his ears when he was told that he had been given a government sponsorship! Was he hearing correctly or had his recent accident damaged his understanding?

While he had been at school, there had been no one to give him any advice or guidance about further education or future career. As a result of this, Kabanda had applied for one of the cheaper courses, just in case he could earn enough to put himself through university one day. He was so amazed to now learn he had won one of the coveted places at university. It was the first and only one awarded to a student from the school at Lugazi!

An overwhelming sense of the goodness and faithfulness of his God swept over him. God had done this! It was due to God's hand on his life and was nothing less than a miracle.

Kabanda wanted so much to hear if his classmates had also done well, but as the school was a boarding one and they all lived in different areas, they could not meet immediately. Sadly, although some had passed the exams, they could not go on to further education because their parents had no money to pay for them.

When the news reached Britain, Hugh and Derek were able to rejoice with Kabanda, and there were many congratulations.

'I knew you could make it!' was Hugh's comment.

How far this boy had come since the day he was left for dead in the ditch!

Kabanda's natural parents were also thrilled. It gave another opportunity for him to share with them that the Lord was real and alive and that he did have a plan for the lives of his children and did help those who put their trust in him. They began to understand a little more why their son had turned to faith in Jesus. To Kabanda's great joy, his brother who was just a little older than him was so touched and amazed by all that God had done for his brother that he accepted Jesus into his own life and became a committed Christian.

The rest of the holiday flew by as now Kabanda could prepare more and more for further studies, with the assurance that he was really going to Makerere University, Kampala.

During that long vacation, Hugh came back to Africa, but not to Uganda. He led a summer mission team to Rwanda for three weeks. He invited Kabanda to travel to Rwanda and join the team to experience mission in a different country. A bus service races between the two countries, and it is a test of faith just to travel that way! In Kigali, Kabanda joined the team, who were working with the Episcopal church under the guidance of the Rev Nathan Amooti.

This was Kabanda's first time in another country, and the beautiful 'land of a thousand hills', as Rwanda is fondly nicknamed, was an amazing place to visit. Rwanda was in recovery after the genocide of 1994 and needed help to rebuild physically, spiritually and emotionally.

It was the first time that Kabanda had been on such a mission team, and he found it a challenging but thrilling experience. There were opportunities to help with practical projects such as building schools and visiting families of orphans from the genocide that were headed by children.

Within Kabanda rose the longing to help the poor and those who were in pain. That trip was a defining point in his life, where he recognised that the Lord wanted him to serve those who were hurting. God had protected and preserved his life in order that he might be a witness to and advocate for the poor.

The mission team consisted of people from the UK led by Hugh and his wife, Marie. Coming from various backgrounds and with ages ranging from 16 to over 60, it represented a huge cross section of life, and from this group Kabanda made friends who have continued to encourage him.

It was here that I first met this remarkable young man, and it has been my joy to see him grow and mature through the years since.

His testimony was such a blessing to all of us, but so were ours to him. The time in Rwanda became a learning time, as Kabanda saw others who had survived different but also terrible experiences in their lives and were learning to trust the Lord. In many places, as we travelled around the country, he was able to share his testimony, and the Lord used it in the hearts of those who heard.

To hear what God had done for Kabanda was especially encouraging to young people in Rwanda who were struggling to get an education and could see no way forward. There were also children who had received terrible injuries in the genocide, and because Kabanda had also experienced terrible injuries, which he would show them by rolling up his trouser leg, they were prepared to listen to what he had to say.

When it was time to return to Uganda, several people on the team had been led to give him clothes, shoes and pocket money to start him off in university, and his heart overflowed with praise and gratitude. One of the greatest joys had been for him to meet Marie, Hugh's wife, for the first time. This was his British Mum! He proudly presented his adoptive parents with a richly embroidered shirt and a dress from Uganda as tokens of his love and gratitude.

This was the first of several times when Kabanda would join mission teams, and doing this has played a significant part in his life since that first visit, helping him to share his story and reach out to others in need. The friendships he made with team members have endured too, and several committed to pray for him and help him when they could.

16 University

Kabanda Nelson was enrolled in Makerere University, Kampala, on 26 September 2002 to embark on a three-year course for a BA degree in social science. It was an amazing achievement, and one that his extended family could hardly take in. It was so far removed from anything ever achieved in the family before and stood as a testimony to his faith as a Christian.

At first it was hard to find a place to live. Only the tuition fees were paid by the government, so Kabanda needed to find money for board and lodging. Halls of residence are reserved for the sons and daughters of the wealthy, so there was no possibility of going there.

Although he had worked hard all his life, Kabanda found it was not easy to get a job in Kampala that would fit in with the lectures at the university. God had provided a place in university, so he knew that God would have somewhere for him to live. He kept on praying, although he was feeling worried as the time drew near to begin and he still had no roof over his head.

So often, it seems, the Lord tests us and leaves the answer to our prayers until the very last minute. Just as Kabanda was despairing, news came from Hugh in Scotland telling him that one of the friends he had made in that first mission trip had sent £50 for his support!

With that money, he was able to secure a place in a student hostel not too far from the campus. The money enabled him to stay there for the first year. It was not the best hostel to lodge in because it was located near a swamp that was infested with a lot of mosquitoes. It meant that

Kabanda did suffer from frequent attacks of malaria, but he persevered and studied hard in order to pass his first-year exams well.

The money ran out after that first year, so Kabanda decided to move out of the capital city and to the small town of Mukono, which was near his home village. Here he was able to rent a room with shared washroom and cookhouse.

In order to support himself, with the help of Hugh and the new friend he had made on the summer team, he was able to set up a little shop in a tiny room on the high street. In it he had basic stationery supplies, a computer and printer and eventually a photocopier. He called it Henderson Computers.

It was hard to both get the business going and then to make it pay, for there were other such places in the town that were already established. He tried to be competitive in his pricing but still be able to make a small profit. He made just about enough money to pay his rent and food and in due course was able to pay a small wage to a young lady who did word processing.

Things seemed to be a little better for Kabanda until one of his brothers became jealous and attacked the shop, breaking equipment and stealing his lifeline, the mobile phone. It was a huge blow and caused him much distress.

How did you deal with such animosity from your own family? It was very difficult to do it the Christian way and to 'turn the other cheek' in forgiveness.

Once again, Kabanda needed a little help from the friends he had made on the mission team, and the business continued to support him throughout his university days. It was a struggle to balance his work, studies and the constant travel to and from Makerere University. He was determined to get as good grades as he possibly could, but it was hard.

Throughout this time, Kabanda was attending a church in Mukono, and the friends there helped and encouraged him. He needed that fellowship because there were times when it would have been easy to become really depressed. Living back at Mukono helped his health as rent was cheaper, which meant he could buy more food, but it was also such a long way to travel each day to classes.

It was the travelling which again caused him trouble. Almost unbelievably, while in his second year at university, Kabanda was involved in yet another road accident. Was the prophecy of some of his family true? Was he to survive two accidents only to die in a third?

Kabanda was walking home after a lecture at university when a car appeared, seemingly from nowhere, and ploughed into him. Again, it was quite a severe accident, and Kabanda was admitted to hospital. He is unable to remember much about it all; he just remembers waking up in the ward. One minute he had been walking along the road, the next moment brought pain and waking up in hospital.

It happened a week before the internal exams for the university year were to be held. Kabanda was quite badly injured, and the medical staff wanted him to remain in hospital for at least two weeks, but he was so distressed that he decided to discharge himself and try to sit the exams. He felt he just could not miss them or he might be sent away from the course, and that would be disastrous.

One of the injuries had been to his right eye, and it caused him a great deal of trouble and pain as he tried to focus on reading the question papers, but with God's help, he managed to complete the exams.

God's timing is amazing, for one of the friends Kabanda had made on the mission team was back in Rwanda and, while knowing nothing of this latest problem, had sent a gift to him through a pastor. The gift arrived at just the right time and was enough to pay the hospital bill. So once again, God had faithfully provided for his son.

Kabanda's friends and family were shocked to hear of yet another accident. To survive three major accidents in a country such as Uganda was such an amazing miracle! That in itself was a testimony to the power of God in this young man's life!

Kabanda could share many incidents of the way in which the Lord provided for him and helped him through his years in university—the times of struggle, the times of joy, the times when faith was weak and the times of answered prayer and encouragement.

He successfully finished his course in 2005 and waited to see how the Lord would open up the way into his future. His one desire was to serve with a grateful heart the God who saw this poor Muslim child left for dead in a ditch and had plans for him, to give him a hope and a future!

Hugh's comment when I asked him about Kabanda's story was, 'When I think back to that night, travelling in the torrential rain, frustrated at a wasted journey and then coming upon Kabanda left for dead in that ditch, I marvel. Who but our great God could put together two such negatives and make such a wonderful positive!'

19 Kabanda's postscript

After graduating from Makerere University, I was so full of happiness, as were my family, who decided to throw a graduation party for me. There was great excitement as this was a 'first' for our family. My parents invited all our many relatives plus our friends to congratulate me on the huge achievement of successfully obtaining a degree.

What they did not take into consideration was that the number of people you invite to such a party should match with the resources available to cater for them! Over 500 guests were invited, and then about another 200 people came who had not been given invitations. This meant that there were not enough chairs, let alone food for everyone.

For me, the most disappointing part of it all was that there was no cake for this party. A family friend who had offered to contribute a graduation cake for the festivities did not fulfil his promise. Halfway through the party, he broke the bad news that he had not received the funds he had expected to be given to buy the cake! This was so disappointing, but it was too late to remedy the situation, so the party continued without a cake.

After my graduation, a new reality set in. Life was not as easy as I had expected it would be once I had successfully gained my degree. I had thought that things would flow very smoothly and my life would be wonderful after university; but the reality did not meet my expectation. I expected that it would be easy to find a good job, maybe buy a car and drive myself to work, get married and start a family and live in a good place in Kampala, Uganda's capital city. Little did I know that there was another mountain for me to climb!

The mountain was called 'The hurdle of finding a job'. Firstly, I had no idea on how to begin searching for a job, and there were no close relatives to guide me in this matter. Secondly, the jobs were just not available. I later learnt that the unemployment rate in Uganda stands around 70%, and it is estimated that each year only 30% of graduates from universities will manage to secure a job.

In a short while, all the excitement of my graduation from university vanished. I discovered that most of the friends who had graduated with me had relatives working for the government or in the private sector, and these relatives secured jobs for them. Their jobs had been handed to them on a plate. All they could do was to advise me to apply for jobs, read the newspapers and look out for vacant positions being advertised.

There is a popular saying in Uganda: 'Technical know "who" is better than technical know "how"', or as it is said in the UK, 'It's not what you know but who you know that counts.'

The challenge was that firstly, it cost money to buy a newspaper, which I did not have, and secondly, most of the posts were advertised as a mere formality, because they had already been filled by people who had relatives 'in the know'. However, I persevered and continued applying but without success. I wrote application after application but was never called for an interview or given the opportunity to meet an employer and talk about my abilities.

This became so frustrating that even my parents lost hope in me getting work and wondered what misfortune was following me! They had thought that I was the one to fulfil their hopes of an improved lifestyle, but it was not happening.

To sustain my daily living, I survived on the small donations from Aunt Mary and a few other UK friends, sent out to me via Dad Hugh. I used that money for rent, food, newspapers and other essentials. It threw me back on God, and I kept praying for the miracle of finding a job.

As my job search continued to be fruitless, I slid down the slope into discouragement until one day when God brought a new friend into my life. At that time, I was making just a small amount of money, using a computer, printer and photocopier which Dad Hugh had bought me. I rented a tiny shack as a duka (little shop) where I could print letters or photocopy documents for a small charge.

Simon came from Ireland to Uganda for two weeks' holiday. He came in one day and asked me to photocopy some papers for him, which I was happy to do. When he asked for the bill, he was surprised because it was so inexpensive. Then he questioned me as to how I could make a living as I charged so little for my work.

As we discussed things further, he suggested that I could become much more competitive in the job market if I did an additional course in accountancy. He suggested a course called ACCA. This is a professional qualification, normally pursued by people who are already working in accountancy.

I applied to a college in Kampala to take this course as an evening class and was given a place. Then I spoke to Dad Hugh in Scotland as well as a few other UK friends, and they were willing to support me through this course.

I began the course, and it gave me an opportunity to meet many professionals working in accountancy and to have a chance to make some friends with my classmates. The college was one with an excellent reputation, attended by many of the sons and daughters of successful Kampala families who wished to excel as accountants.

Due to my situation where I was not in full employment, I had more time to myself, so I used to arrive early at the college before the other students came.

I was very blessed because one evening a classmate called Paul came in and chatted, telling me that he was surprised to find that I was always in class before anyone else.

'How do you manage that?' he asked me. 'You must finish your work very early and then be able to navigate your way through the traffic jams to arrive here before anyone else.'

'I don't have a job, Paul,' I answered. 'I spend my time studying and come early to college to read.'

Paul was so surprised to learn this, and then he had an idea.

'Would you like me to have a word with my boss and see if he could employ you as my assistant?' he asked.

Would I indeed! I was so excited that I found it hard to concentrate on the class that evening, thinking about the possibility of having a proper job at last! I was unable to sleep that night but spent time praying and asking the Lord that he would make Paul's boss accept the proposal.

The following evening, Paul arrived earlier at college than normal, and as usual I was already there.

'My boss is interested in talking to you and discussing a job offer,' Paul told me.

I was beside myself with excitement. We discussed the details, and the very next morning I dressed in my best clothes and went to the office where Paul worked to have an interview and meet his boss. He worked at a company called UAE Exchange, a subsidiary of a Dubai-based company dealing with money transfers and foreign exchange.

The boss looked at my CV and certificates and liked what he saw.

'How much salary would you like?' he asked me.

'I am happy to work for whatever salary you offer,' I replied. Then he offered me the job!

I was so happy about this opportunity and phoned my parents at once to tell them the good news, which they quickly spread around family and friends.

This was my first step into formal employment. I thanked God so much for this opportunity—the first rung of the ladder! It felt great to be like the rest of my classmates at college, going to work for the day and then heading out to the class.

I continued to study and work hard, indeed with extra enthusiasm now that I could see that my future was becoming brighter. It was another achievement in my life, and I glorified God for it. In time I obtained both ACCA and MBA qualifications.

I knew now that it was time to give support and make a difference in my large family. Even though my starting salary was small, I was determined to help them somehow. I visited the village and discussed with my parents the best way to help my many siblings. Unfortunately, it was too late to help most of my generation because they had left school and were engaged in small, 'dead end' casual jobs, and some had already married and were struggling to bring up families.

In our culture, it seems a sad thing that when a person is unable to get much of an education, they opt for an early marriage. I was saddened that I could not help my sisters because they had all dropped out of school and married in the hope that their husbands might take care of them.

My brothers too had given up on school and had already started families and had children whom they were unable to support. Because I was determined to make a change in my family, I realised that the next best thing was to support my nephews and nieces and then any other family member that I could.

The first group of children whose support I took on were the three children of my brother who had sadly died, leaving them orphaned— they were all under six years of age. We held a family meeting after his funeral and decided to jointly support and raise these three children, giving them the opportunity to go to school. In the end it turned out that I was the only one undertaking to do this, because all my relatives were struggling financially trying to support their own families.

I thank God for his provision and that I have been able to support these children, and two of the three are now in the final year of secondary school. I pray that I will be enabled to continue their support so that they are able to progress to university.

There are also some other nephews and nieces for whom I am able to help pay school fees because I have learnt the value of education and how it has the ability to change life's circumstances.

My position as a wage earner also means that I am the one to whom family members turn when they have sudden emergencies such as hospital admissions or operations or when they need small loans to start a little business. This brings both a burden and a joy. For example, one of the family members whom I am supporting is at university doing an engineering degree. It is an expensive course, but

I want him to complete it in the hope that he will then be able to help others once he gets work.

At times, it is hard to make the family budget stretch, but I tell the students whom I support one thing—I do not expect a payback, but I do ask them that once they have finished school and are employed that they follow my example and do for others what I have done for them. I fully support eight students at the present time and partially support a couple of others. I am just so thankful to the Lord for his provision.

Once I had successfully finished the ACCA course, I was able to apply for and be successful in getting a better-paid job as well as able to do some extra business. This meant that I was financially secure enough to look for a wife and begin my own family. It was then that I met Florence, who agreed to become my dear wife.

Our wedding ceremonies are different from those in Britain. A formal wedding in Uganda begins with the 'Introduction' wedding in which the bride and bridegroom's family negotiate the bride price which the groom has to provide, usually in a certain number of live cows. It is all done with an audience of wider family and friends, along with a feast. There is a lot of haggling—all in fun, as the price will have been agreed before this event.

The second part of a 'formal wedding' is the civil ceremony, and then, for Christian couples, the third part is a church wedding and reception.

I was the first to have a formal marriage within the family, so my parents were not able to guide me, but some of my friends whom I had met through my studies had already married, and they could advise me in all that was involved in preparing for such a wedding.

Kabanda's postscript

We were married on 21 November 2015 at Ggaba Community Church in Kampala, a beautiful wedding attended by 500 invited guests. The reception was held in one of Kampala's best hotels, which one of my friends had previously used for his reception.

With much support from friends and workmates, I was able to have a colourful wedding party.

Among the key guests were Dad Hugh and Derek, to whom I owe so much, especially for leading me to Jesus, and Simon, who now lives in London and flew over with his wife Alexandra. Florence and I were so thrilled to have such a wonderful wedding.

We are full of thanks because God has been so gracious to us—as of 2022, our family has now grown as we have two daughters (Skyla and Tyra) and a son (Harley), and we live in our own house in Bweyogerere, thirteen kilometres east of Kampala.

I continue to do some small trade in real estate to supplement my regular salary, and I have experienced God's grace in everything I do. Of late, my colleagues have nicknamed me 'Blessed One'. I give all the glory back to God.

Kabanda Nelson

Author's postscript

Becoming a Christian is only the beginning of an exciting but challenging journey of discipleship whichever culture we live in. That has certainly been the case for Kabanda. In Uganda, there are few opportunities for young people born to parents who have had little formal education, and even when they do succeed as Kabanda did, it is still very difficult to get a good job and earn a reasonable salary.

His diligence and humility, together with his persistence in following Jesus despite much opposition, has made an impact on his Muslim family and friends. One of his brothers is now a committed Christian and serving God. Kabanda's childhood friend, Stephen, who also gave his life to the Lord, is serving as a pastor in a church in Kampala.

Several other family members have professed faith in Christ, but Kabanda has yet to see a real change in their lives. He continues to pray for them and show the love of Christ in his actions. One of his paternal uncles who is a Muslim leader recently came to him and thanked him for the difference he has made in his family.

My prayer is that everyone who reads this story will be challenged to have the courage to live for the Lord whatever circumstances they may have to face and remain faithful throughout their lives.

Blessed is the one who perseveres under trial because, having stood the test, that person will receive the crown of life that the Lord has promised to those who love him. James 1:12

God will bless you if you don't give up when your faith is being tested.

Discussion questions

Chapter 1 Kabanda lived in a very difficult cultural environment, probably very different from most of the readers of this book. Can you think of at least one thing about your upbringing for which you are thankful?

Chapter 2 What are your thoughts about sacrificing animals and consulting witch doctors? How might this differ from using medicines bought from a chemist or health store?

Chapter 3 In African culture you are considered a 'child' until you leave the home and marry, so even in his late teens Kabanda would continue to be submissive to his parents or carer. How well do you get on with other family members? What might you be able to do to strengthen relationships with them? Consider Kabanda and James's relationship.

Chapter 4 How would you feel and possibly react if you were in Kabanda's situation when his first bike was stolen and he was left in the forest?

Chapter 5 'God's ways are beyond our understanding, and he looks for the most crucial moments to show his love' was Kabanda's comment about his terrible accident with the fish truck. What do you think about this statement?

Chapter 6 The story of the 'lost' £20 note in the plaster cast and how God blessed his generosity to the doctor in so many ways has been indelibly imprinted on Kabanda's memory. Can you think of a time when God provided for a need you had?

Chapter 7 Life became very hard for Kabanda when he returned to the village and was pressurised to abandon his faith. Have there been times when you felt like giving up your faith? What enabled you to continue?

Chapter 8 The Muslim Imam hated Kabanda and was verbally abusive to him. What is your attitude towards people who hold different and possibly anti-Christian views?

Chapter 9 Going to the Lugazi school should have been wonderful for Kabanda, but it proved less than that. How might you have reacted in a similar circumstance—when someone who should have protected you let you down?

Chapter 10 Kabanda felt abandoned and depressed. Christians are not immune from such times. Where would you go for help and support?

Chapter 11 Kabanda's fears about his leg falling off proved unfounded. We all have fears in times of severe or unexpected illness. Do you believe or have you experienced God's divine intervention and healing?

Chapter 12 Derek's visit to Lugazi brought new hope and joy to Kabanda. Christian friendship and fellowship should mean so much— are you a good listener and friend, and can you share your needs with others? If not, what hinders you?

Chapter 13 Kabanda's work ethic and attitudes were a good example to his school mates. How can our lives encourage others?

Chapter 14 The temptation to cheat was huge. Can you think of any time when you felt a strong temptation, and how did you cope?

Chapter 15. We all want our plans to work out—when they don't, how should we react?

Chapter 16 Even when God has granted our heart's desire, life can still be difficult. What can we learn from Kabanda in order to stay steadfast in our faith?

Kabanda's postscript

1. How would you feel about having to support your younger family members financially or other members of your extended family if they were in financial need once you had a regular salary?

2. Jeremiah 29:11 is a wonderful verse, and it has helped many Christians down through the ages. How can we find God's plan for our lives at every age and stage, so that John 10:10 can be true in our experience?

Hugh and Kabanda

Running the shop while at university

**Kabanda and Florence's
wedding at Ggaba Community
Church in 2015**

The boy, the bike and the fish truck

Visiting Murchinson Falls Game Park as a treat for Christmas 2021 — Harley, Florence, Skyla and Kabanda

Birth of Tyra (meaning 'God is the God of battle') in June 2022